TRAEGER GRILL & SMOKER COOKBOOK

Your Final Grill and Smoke Recipe Bible. Become A Master of a Wood Pellet Grill. Healthy and Delicious Recipes for Complete Beginners and More Advanced Cooks.

TABLE OF CONTENTS

INTRODUCTION 8

CHAPTER 1: WHAT IS A TRAEGER GRILL & SMOKER?.................................. 10

How Does it Work? 11

CHAPTER 2: WHY CHOOSE TRAEGER GRILL 12

CHAPTER 3: BENEFITS OF TRAEGER GRILL 14

Ease of Use 14
Versatile 14
Even Cooking 15
Regulating the Temperature 15
The Texture and Juiciness Increase.. 15
Nutrients Are not Lost 15
A Spectacular Flavor 15
Your Dishes Contain less Fat 15
Ideal for Family Meals or with a Large Number of People............................... 15
The Disadvantages of Grilling 16

CHAPTER 4: DIFFERENT TYPES OF TRAEGER GRILL 18

CHAPTER 5: ACCESSORIES AND EXTRA 20

CHAPTER 6: WHAT ARE PELLETS?... 22

Anatomy of A Pellet Grill... 23
Wood Pellets 24

CHAPTER 7: WHAT CAN YOU COOK?.. 26

Pork 27
Beef 28
Poultry 30
Lamb 31
Fish.. 33

CHAPTER 8: USEFUL TIPS FOR GRILL TRAEGER USERS............................. 34

Tips and Tricks... 35
Store your Pellets Properly 36
Wrap Thermocouple with Aluminum Foil to Prevent Grease Build-up 36
Cover the Grill when not in Use 36
Clean Grill Regularly 36
Try out New Recipes and Utilize Every Function 36
Pellet Storage 36
Temperature Readings 36
Cover Your Grill 37
Cooking Temperatures, Times, and Doneness 37

CHAPTER 9: DIFFERENT TYPES OF COOKING 40

Components of Wood Pellet Grill and their Functions 41

CHAPTER 10: HOW TO PROPERLY CLEAN THE TRAEGER GRILL AND MAINTENANCE........... 44

Hardwood Pallets 45
Hopper... 45

CONTROLLER 45

INDUCTION FAN 45

AUGER... 45

HOT ROD 45

FIREPOT 45

DRIP TRAY 45

CHAPTER 11: BREAKFAST **48**

CORNED BEEF HASH 50

TURKEY SANDWICH 51

SCRAMBLED EGGS 51

BERRY SMOOTHIE 52

AVOCADO SMOOTHIE 52

TOFU SMOOTHIE 53

BANANA NUT OATMEAL 54

CARROT STRAWBERRY SMOOTHIE 54

GREEN SMOOTHIE 55

KID-FRIENDLY ZUCCHINI BREAD 56

BREAKFAST SAUSAGE CASSEROLE 57

KETO QUICHE 58

CHAPTER 12: BEEF RECIPES **60**

SMOKED AND PULLED BEEF 61

WOOD PELLET SMOKED BEEF JERKY 61

REVERSE SEARED FLANK STEAK 62

SMOKED MIDNIGHT BRISKET 63

GRILLED BUTTER BASTED PORTERHOUSE STEAK 64

COCOA CRUSTED GRILLED FLANK STEAK 64

WOOD PELLET GRILL PRIME RIB ROAST 65

SMOKED LONGHORN COWBOY TRI-TIP 66

WOOD PELLET GRILL TERIYAKI BEEF JERKY 66

GRILLED BUTTER BASTED RIB-EYE 67

WOOD PELLET SMOKED BRISKET 68

TRAEGER BEEF JERKY 69

TRAEGER SMOKED BEEF ROAST 69

REVERSE SEARED FLANK STEAK 70

TRAEGER BEEF TENDERLOIN 71

TRAGER NEW YORK STRIP 71

TRAEGER STUFFED PEPPERS 72

TRAEGER PRIME RIB ROAST 73

FINE INDIAN SMOKED T-BONE 74

THE SOUTH BARBACOA 74

SMOKED PRIME RIB 75

KOREAN BEEF RIB EYE 76

CHAPTER 13: POULTRY RECIPES **78**

LEMON CHICKEN 79

HONEY GARLIC CHICKEN WINGS 79

CAJUN CHICKEN 80

CHILI BARBECUE CHICKEN 80

SERRANO CHICKEN WINGS 81

SMOKED FRIED CHICKEN 82

MAPLE TURKEY BREAST 83

CHICKEN TIKKA MASALA 83
TURKEY WITH APRICOT BARBECUE GLAZE 84
TURKEY MEATBALLS 84
HERB ROASTED TURKEY 85
TURKEY LEGS 86
TURKEY BREAST 87
SPICY BBQ CHICKEN 88
TERIYAKI WINGS 88

CHAPTER 14: FISH RECIPES 90

JERK SHRIMP 91
SPICY SHRIMPS SKEWERS 91
TUNA TACOS 92
LEMON GARLIC SCALLOPS 93
HALIBUT IN PARCHMENT 94
CHILEAN SEA BASS 94
SRIRACHA SALMON 95
GRILLED RAINBOW TROUT 96
CIDER SALMON 97
OCTOPUS WITH LEMON AND OREGANO 98
MUSSELS WITH PANCETTA AÏOLI 99
MANGO SHRIMP 100
BLACKENED SALMON 100
BLACKENED CATFISH 101
BACON-WRAPPED SCALLOPS 102
CAJUN SEASONED SHRIMP 102
JUICY SMOKED SALMON 103

CHAPTER 15: VEGETABLE RECIPES 104

GRILLED GREEN BEANS 105
GRILLED ASPARAGUS 105
TRAEGER GRILL EGGPLANTS 106
GREEN BEANS WITH BACON 106
GRILLED POTATO SALAD 107
VEGETABLE SANDWICH 108
GRILLED ZUCCHINI 109
GRILLED SUGAR SNAP PEAS 109
CAULIFLOWER WITH PARMESAN AND BUTTER 110
GRILLED CARROTS AND ASPARAGUS 111
KALE CHIPS 111
BACON-WRAPPED JALAPEÑO POPPERS 112
ROASTED PARMESAN CHEESE BROCCOLI 113

CHAPTER 16: LAMB AND GOAT RECIPES 114

LAMB KABOBS 115
GRILLED PORK CHOPS 115
GRILLED LAMB LIVER 116
ROASTED LEG OF LAMB 117
GRILLED LAMB KABOBS 117
BRAISED LAMB SHANK 118
SMOKED LAMB LEG WITH SALSA VERDE 119
GRILLED LAMB CHOPS WITH ROSEMARY 120
BISON TOMAHAWK STEAK 120

BRAISED ELK SHANK 121

BAKED VENISON MEATLOAF 122

ROASTED VENISON TENDERLOIN 122

GRILLED VENISON KABOB 123

SWEETHEART STEAK 124

BLOODY MARY FLANK STEAK 124

TRAEGER GRILL ROSEMARY LAMB WITH GARLIC 125

RACK OF LAMB 126

MOUTHWATERING LAMB CHOPS 126

GREEK LAMB LEG 127

MOROCCAN LAMB RIBS 128

CHAPTER 17: PORK RECIPES **130**

SMOKED BABY BACK RIBS 131

SMOKED APPLE PORK TENDERLOIN 131

COMPETITION STYLE BBQ PORK RIBS 132

SMOKED APPLE BBQ RIBS 133

CITRUS-BRINED PORK ROAST 133

PORK COLLAR AND ROSEMARY MARINADE 134

ROASTED HAM 135

SMOKED PORK LOIN 135

SMOKE PULLED PORK 136

EASY PORK CHUCK ROAST 137

PINEAPPLE PORK BBQ 138

BBQ SPARERIBS WITH MANDARIN GLAZE 138

SMOKED PORK SAUSAGES 139

BRAISED PORK CHILE VERDE 140

BBQ PULLED PORK SANDWICHES 141

CONCLUSION **142**

Introduction

Traeger is the premium wood pellet grill. A grill that will allow you to transfer your kitchen to the backyard for the summer. In fact, the Traeger doesn't just allow you to smoke and grill but also bake and cook. And you can use it any time of the year to give an extra smoky kick to any dish you want.

Why don't surprise your family with a perfectly smoked Thanksgiving Turkey? Why don't delight your children with Sunday morning breakfast with apple-smoked bacon? And how about a long day of enjoying beers with your friend waiting for that perfectly juicy Texas-style brisket-You can craft an entire woodfired meal from start to finish with the flip of a switch, thanks to the Traeger technology. This book will guide you through all the methods and techniques to fully utilize your Traeger. From maintenance to smoking techniques, from pulled pork to brownies: this is the complete guide to the best wood pellet grill money can buy.

The wood pellet grill was born from something all of us have experienced at one time or another: failure.

A failed meal on an inferior grill was all it took for Joe Traeger to turn the outdoor cooking world on its head. He became the inventor of the pellet grill and founder of Traeger Pellet Grills. The wood pellet grill gave everyday consumers masterful results by removing the guesswork from the barbecue and eliminating unwanted flare-ups and flames.

Since the introduction of the wood pellet grill in the mid-1980s, its use has spread across North America, giving customers enhanced temperature control and woodfired flavor in each meal.

On top of the moist results it delivers every time, the woodfired flavor has made the pellet grill a coveted item for everyone—from world-champion pit masters to the weekend backyard warrior.

Over the years, the methods of achieving these moist, delicious meals have changed as more advanced controllers and drain systems, as well as adjustments in the augers and burn area, have been introduced.

New designs, including Wi-Fi control boards and direct flame searing, are all the rage today. Though the design has evolved, each pellet grill aims for the same result: amazing wood-fired flavor without the hassle of a direct flame.

Whether you have a Traeger grill or are considering buying one, we will guide you through an amazing journey to smoking meats, grilling fish, and beyond... If you try cooking with real wood, you will never want to go back!

CHAPTER 1:

What is a Traeger Grill & Smoker?

Pellet grills are outdoor cookers that utilize modern technologies to ignite all-natural hardwood pellets as a fuel source for heating and cooking your food. They are an electric-powered, automated device for precisely cooking your food with delicious wood-fired taste.

Most pellet grills have temperature ranges near 200°F-500°F, which is an ample range to handle hot searing grill jobs as well as low and slow smoking.

Aesthetically, they look something like a cross between a standard barrel-style grill and an offset smoker.

An important note about your pellet grill – it does not cook with direct heat. Pellet grills have a deflector plate that distributes heat around the cooking chamber, where air and heat flow similar to a convection oven. This is exactly why it's possible to also bake and roast on your pellet grill.

You might also hear people refer to these cookers as both a "pellet grill" and a "pellet smoker". For many cookers, the difference between being referred to as a "grill" or a "smoker" is huge. In the case of pellet grills though, they're the same

This type of smoker grill is known to cook food using all-nature wood pellets so that foods do not only smell and taste great but also healthy. But unlike traditional smokers, the Traeger Grill has been innovated to provide convenience even to grill and barbecue neophytes. It comes with a motor that turns the auger thereby consistently feeding the burn pot so you can achieve even cooking.

This innovative grill allows you to cook authentic grilled foods yet you don't deviate from the tradition of cooking using wood pellets so you don't get that distasteful aftertaste you get from cooking in a gas grill.

Made by an Oregon-based company, the Traeger Grill has been around for many decades. This type of smoker grill is known to cook food using all-nature wood pellets so that foods do not only smell and taste great but also healthy. But unlike traditional smokers, the Traeger Grill has been innovated to provide convenience even to grill and barbecue neophytes. It comes with a motor that turns the auger thereby consistently feeding the burn pot so you can achieve even cooking.

How Does it Work?

The wood pellets are placed in the auger from the hopper. For higher temperatures, more wood pellets are added to the auger. The auger then transfers the wood pallets to the firepot where a fire is burning. The firepot makes the hotrod ignite the piece of wood, and smoke and fire from the wood are released. A drip tray stands just right on top of the hotrod and the burning wood to stop the naked flame. A fan inside the device is turned on, and it evenly distributes the smoke and heat to the food on top of the grill. For precise temperature controls, some grills are now equipped with an app that helps the cook control the temperature per his or her needs.

The Traeger wood pallets grill not only grills but also can be used for baking, smoking, roasting, and braising.

CHAPTER 2:

Why Choose Traeger Grill

The Traeger Grill is not only limited to, well, grilling. It is an essential outdoor kitchen appliance as it allows you to also bake, roast, smoke, braise, and barbecue. But more than it is a useful kitchen appliance, below are the advantages of getting your very own Traeger Grill:

Better flavor: The Traeger Grill uses all-natural wood, so food comes out better-tasting compared to when you cook them in a gas or charcoal grill. There are 14 different flavors that you can impart to your food and this book will have its chapter dedicated to those 14 flavors of pellets.

No flare-ups: No flare-ups mean that food is cooked evenly on all sides. This is made possible by using indirect heat. And because there are no flare-ups, you can smoke, bake, and rise without some areas or sides of your food burning.

Mechanical parts are well designed and protected: The mechanical parts of the Traeger Grill are protected particularly from fats and drippings, so it does not get stuck over time.

Exceptional temperature control: The Traeger Grill has exceptional temperature control. The thing is that all you need is to set up the heat and the grill will maintain a consistent temperature even if the weather goes bad. Moreover, having a stable temperature control allows you to cook food better and tastier minus the burnt taste.

Built-in Wi-Fi: All Traeger Grills have built-in Wi-Fi so you can set them up even if you are not physically present in front of your grill. Moreover, the grill also alerts you once your food is ready. With this setting, you will be able to do other important things instead of slaving in front of your grill. Lastly, it also comes with an app that allows you to check many recipes from their website.

Environmentally friendly: Perhaps the main selling point of the Traeger Grill is that it is environmentally friendly. Traeger Grill uses all-natural wood pellets, so your grill does not produce harmful chemicals when you are using it... only smoky goodness.

The thing is that the Traeger Grill is more than just your average grill. It is one of the best there is, and you will get your money's worth with this grill.

CHAPTER 3:

Benefits of Traeger Grill

To help you enjoy the best of cooking experience and ensure that you truly bring out the best in the recipes, we are going to talk about some of the best tips and tricks that you can make use of.

However, just before that, we want to familiarize you with the key benefits which the use of wood pellet grills has to offer. Make sure to optimize the most out of it.

Ease of Use

Compared to smokers and even other cooking methods, there is no denying the fact that wood pellet grills offer remarkable ease of use. You can simply feed in the controls and relax and enjoy the meals.

Versatile

The use of wood pellet grills will ensure that you will be able to cook a wide variety of food. There is going to be a massive variety as these grills aren't limited to meat alone. From braised short ribs to poultry, beef, and red meat, chicken, and more; there are a whole lot of things you can work on.

Even Cooking

There is no doubt that these grills let you have a very even style of cooking. This, in turn, makes sure that the quality of food is top-notch.

Regulating the Temperature

With wood pellet grills, you don't need to babysit the whole time. When it comes to regulating the temperature, the controller will take care of it. With the traditional grills, this is often the most tedious task in the cooking process.

The Texture and Juiciness Increase

Cooking on the grill ensures a uniform temperature that gives our meats unrivaled juiciness that is not grilled or baked. But you have to know several tricks to make them look tenderer than ever. The first of these is to close the grill lid or cover this meat with pot lids or metal pans. This will make the heat spread evenly and we can enjoy a texture like no other.

Another trick is to avoid cutting the meat or pressing it while it is on the grill because this way it can lose its texture and be much drier. And finally, the third tip is to let the meat rest for at least ten minutes, once cooked. This will keep it juicier and retain the flavor better.

Nutrients Are not Lost

With this cooking technique, the nutrients found in your food will not be lost and will remain intact throughout the cooking. This will lead to healthier and more nutritious dishes. And in this way, you will take care of yourself much more!

A Spectacular Flavor

The flavor of your vegetables or your grilled or grilled meats is one of the main advantages of why choose this cooking technique and not others. You will not need to use sauces and condiments, as the grill will enhance the flavor of the food itself. And forget about adding extra calories!

Your Dishes Contain less Fat

Dishes prepared on the grill are lighter and healthier. But why? Well, these foods tend to have less fat since they are only cooked in their natural fat and it is not necessary to add other types of oils or butter, which in other forms of cooking we do need. Besides, most of the fat in your grilled meats often sheds and falls off during cooking, making this fat not stick to or stay around the food.

Ideal for Family Meals or with a Large Number of People

This is because a grill supports more ingredients and all kinds of food. It is perfect for not being soaked in the kitchen for hours and hours on some birthday or special date in which many people have to eat. You can vary the ingredients, introduce all kinds of vegetables and greens, red beef or pork, or white meats such as chicken, the latter being the healthiest option you can use.

Make sure that the raw meats you have on your grill do not come into contact with vegetables, as there may be contamination.

The Disadvantages of Grilling

Like all high-temperature cooking, grilling leads to the formation of Maillard compounds which give food a colored appearance. These compounds are toxic and can be carcinogenic. To limit the formation of these compounds, it is preferable to have the cooking time as short as possible.

CHAPTER 4:

Different Types of Traeger Grill

Along with the wood pellet grills, if you would also like to know a little about the types of BBQ, here is a consolidated list that can come in handy.

Gas Grills These grills tend to mostly run on natural gas or bottled propane. They are suited for backyard cooking as they tend to produce a great deal of smoke. It does have great ease of use and tends to heat up very quickly. But the food is likely to miss out on the characteristic smokey flavor. So, if you are a diehard BBQ fan, this might not be the best option for you.

Charcoal Grills They tend to mostly make use of charcoal briquettes as the source of fuel. Unlike the gas grills, they will give you the authentic taste of BBQ and will enhance the actual taste of the food. There are a few drawbacks to using this grill as the use of charcoal as a source of fuel turns out to be expensive. Along with this, the cleaning of grills is a tedious affair as well.

Electric Grills These grills use the electric source as a means to get fired up. It is also suited for indoor use as it doesn't require any external flame. It, therefore, doesn't lead to any kind of unwanted pollution, and at the same time, the food tends to be cooked fast. It is more suited for city people who have several rules to abide by regarding the use of gas and charcoal as a fuel source. However, once again, the typical woody and smokey flavor may be missing owing to the lack of use of wooden pallets.

Portable Grills These grills can be easily moved from one place to the other and are extremely popular for the portability factor. It is great when you are looking to go camping and you can set your grill and fire it up and cook food as and when you want.

While they are an excellent choice, you need to know that this might not be the best choice for large parties as it can cook a limited amount of food in one go.

So, these are the different types of BBQ and you can decide the ones that seem to be apt for you. With all these details, we believe that you are now ready for the recipes.

When following the recipes, make it a point to adhere to the instructions as closely you can. The key thing about wood pellet smoker recipes is using the right pellets, controlling the temperature, and following the cooking instructions. Every detail is important and will have a role to play as far as infusing the dish with the perfect flavor is concerned.

CHAPTER 5:

Accessories and Extra

Some accessories are essential and are must-haves to have a fantastic experience with Wood Pellet Grill Smokers. There are several grilling accessories in their thousands; however, there are certain ones that are non-negotiable if you want to get the best from your Pellet Smoker. The purpose of these accessories is to make things easier and, in other cases, serve as protection.

Grilling Tools

Some tools are specially designed for grilling purposes. They are usually more robust and sturdier than the regular kitchen utensils. Some of these tools include; spatula, tongs, fork, *etc.*

Heat-resistant Gloves

Everyone loves having a barbecue party. But while you are at it, you want to make sure you do not burn your hands. Getting a pair of heat-resistant gloves will go a long way to protect you from the fire's scorching heat.

Basting Brush and the Sauce Mop

These tools are essential to prevent dry-out. When grilling, the tools help to add moisture after the barbecue has formed its crust. The brush usually has a long handle, and it's made of silicone for easy cleaning. The sauce mop is more like a bunch of strings attached to a long handle. It becomes easy to reach the back of the pellet smoker with the sauce mop without the risk of burns.

Grill Brush

This tool is essential to keep your cooking area clean. It is recommended to use this after every cook to remove any bristle stuck on your grill grate. Ensure to crank the temperature for about 10 minutes before the cleaning is done.

Cutting Board

A quality cutting board is an essential tool to have as well. It will create a strong base for you to handle your brisket, however large the size is.

Several other helpful tools and accessories are available, although they may not be considered significant. When you invest in the right accessories, they make your grilling experience a smooth and enjoyable one.

CHAPTER 6:

What Are Pellets?

Traeger Wood Pellet Grills are electric grills that use wood pellets as their fuel source. The specially designed wood pellets can also be used as flavor enhancers to give food an excellent smoky taste. With his grill, Joe Traeger revolutionized barbecuing and made it convenient and straightforward. Traeger Wood Pellet Grill and Smoker does not require constant monitoring and can be left to regulate itself while cooking.

Pellet grills are outdoor cookers that utilize modern technologies to ignite all-natural hardwood pellets as a fuel source for heating and cooking your food. They are an electric-powered, automated device for precisely cooking your food with delicious wood-fired taste.

Most pellet grills have temperature ranges near 200°F-500°F, which is an ample range to handle hot searing grill jobs as well as low and slow smoking.

Aesthetically, they look something like a cross between a standard barrel-style grill and an offset smoker.

An important note about your pellet grill – it does not cook with direct heat. Pellet grills have a deflector plate that distributes heat around the cooking chamber, where air and heat flow similar to a convection oven. This is exactly why it's possible to also bake and roast on your pellet grill.

You might also hear people refer to these cookers as both a "pellet grill" and a "pellet smoker". For many cookers, the difference between being referred to as a "grill" or a "smoker" is huge. In the case of pellet grills though, they're the same. Since pellet grills are capable of both grilling and smoking, you'll hear them referred to by both names.

Anatomy of A Pellet Grill

The Hopper

On the side of the pellet grill, you'll find a hopper, which houses your supply of wood pellets. Hopper size varies based on which model of pellet grill you own, but most hold between 10 and 20 pounds of wood pellets at a time.

The hopper has its lid and can be accessed mid cook without opening the lid of your cooking chamber. This way, you can maintain the ambient temperature of your grill even if you need to refill wood pellets in the middle of your cook.

The Digital Controller

The digital controller is what gives pellet grills their ease of use and precision. With the turn of a dial or the press of a button, you can set your temperature just like you would on a traditional oven. An LED display will show your grill's actual temperature so you can know exactly how your food is being cooked.

A sensor probe inside your grill monitors the cooker's ambient temperature. If the temperature falls too low, the controller will distribute more wood pellets down to the fire pot to ignite. This is part of what makes pellet grills so easy to use - they automate temperature management.

Many newer pellet grill models also have built-in probe thermometers, which are one of the most important tools for any grill master. Built-in thermometers will display your food's internal temperature on the LED display alongside your grill's ambient temperature.

The Auger

Pellets that are dispensed by the digital controller fall into an auger, which is a screw-shaped design feature. The auger rotates in place and pushes pellets forward to be fed into the firepot.

The Firepot

After the wood pellets journey through the auger, they are dumped into a firepot. In the firepot, an electric igniter rod heats pellets until they begin to smolder, smoke, and ignite.

Just above the firepot is a deflector plate that distributes heat around the grill. The deflector plate eliminates hot spots and also acts as a shield for the firepot. No drippings, fats, grease, or oils can make their way to the firepot – eliminating the possibility of flare-ups.

The Fan

Pellet grills also come with a built-in fan system to feed oxygen to the firepot. After all, there's no fire without oxygen.

When more heat is required, the digital controller will turn the fan cadence up to increase oxygen flow. This principle is pretty similar to how air dampers and vents work in charcoal grills and smokers.

The Chimney

Typically, on the opposite end from the hopper, there's a chimney that allows smoke to exit the cooking chamber. This creates a draw of airflow to keep heat and smoke flowing properly inside of the cooking chamber. It's also an escape for smoke so that you don't over-smoke your food. There are many reasons to love the pellet grill, but here is a shortlist of my favorites!

The pellet grill is the ultimate versatile outdoor cooker. Grilling, smoking, roasting, baking, and braising are all possible on a pellet grill.

Set it and forget it's the style of the cooker. The digital controller makes every aspect of managing your cook simple, precise, and easy.

Real wood-fired smoke flavor for your food. There's also a very small chance that you can over-do it with smoke flavor on a pellet grill.

Large quantities of food can cook evenly at the same time thanks to convection style cooking.

Wood Pellets

Wood pellets are the fuel source of pellet grills. Essentially, they are compressed capsules of sawdust from repurposed wood. Lumber yards, for example, have a lot of scrap wood that is useless for most practical applications. Pellet grills found a use for this scrap by collecting and pressurizing it into a small wood pellet.

It's important to quickly note the difference between heating pellets and food-grade hardwood pellets for smoking and grilling. Heating pellets can be made from wood that has chemicals and toxins in it – the kind of stuff you'd never want to get into your food. These pellets were designed for old school heating stoves and NOT for pellet grills.

The type of pellets we're talking about are made from 100% all-natural hardwood that is dried out then ground to sawdust. The sawdust is pressurized at extreme heat to create compact pellets, which are then coated and held together.

Hardwood pellets are great because they impart bona fide wood-fired flavor into your food. They also burn quite efficiently and ash at an extremely low rate. For reference, a 40-pound bag of wood pellets will typically produce only about half of a cup of ash.

Different types of wood impart different flavors to your food. Some wood species work best with specific types of food, but half of the fun of outdoor cooking is experimenting! Don't be afraid to try a new wood flavor with your food next time you fire up the grill.

Also, worth noting – you can blend pellets. Many manufacturers sell their own proprietary pellet blend recipes, but nothing is stopping you from blending at home. If you want to soften the flavor of a stronger smoke or simply want to experiment, try different blends, and see how they go.

CHAPTER 7:

What Can you Cook?

Different meat cuts take a specific amount of time. For instance, lean cuts dry out quickly, while the fatty cuts remain moist longer. For this reason, you should always treat a specific cut of meat differently from others.

Below are some of the best meat cuts for smoking;

Beef Brisket Beef brisket is one of the best meat cuts for smoked barbecue. Although it is difficult to get right, it's good marbling and thick, fatty top locks in all the juices, adding more flavor to your meat.

Beef Ribs Located in the area between the brisket and the flank steak, they are the easiest to smoke, and their excellent marbling and fat content help keep the meat moist.

Sirloin Steak It consists of the top and bottom sirloin, and it is located by the steer's hip. Between the two, the top sirloin is more tender, which makes it ideal for smoking.

Flank Steak This is yet another excellent meat cut that is perfect for smoking. In addition to being affordable, it is also easy to prepare, making it a good option for beginners. It comes from the steer's underside, along the animal's side, and close to the belly.

Pork

Pork has a salty flavor that cannot be mistaken. The fat content in pork, though it can get in the way at times, allows it to be both juicy and tender.

Pork goes extremely well with sweet flavors, and I refer to that a lot. Pick up some local honey; it supports the beekeepers, farmers, and markets in the area. Plus, local honey tastes better. Brown sugar is delicious with pork, too. And whenever I visit a buddy in Toronto, I always pick up some Canadian maple syrup in the duty-free shop on the way home to have on hand for pork recipes.

1. **Head**

2. Clear Plate

3. **Back Fat**

4. Boston Butt/Shoulder

5. **Loin/Tenderloin**

6. **Ham**

7. Cheek

8. **Picnic Shoulder**

9. Ribs

10. **Bacon/Belly**

11. **Hock**

RIBS

I am going to speak in general terms when dealing with pork ribs, both spare ribs, and baby backs. In both cases, you want to select a cut with a good amount of fat, but it should be consistent throughout. Too much fat, especially if it is only in certain places, can make for an unappetizing fatty bite.

We are going to prep our ribs the way you see them at a competition, not at the local chain barbecue restaurant. These will have just the slightest pull to them just before the meat slips and falls off the bone. If you want the meat slipping and sliding off the bone, cook them a little longer.

PORK SHOULDER

Pulled pork is something pit masters love. Not just because it's easy and good, but because it typically means leftovers for days. Sliders, nachos, and sandwiches are all day-two and day-three renditions of the pulled-pork-leftover week. A good-size pork shoulder could feed an army—or at least an army of kids just back from baseball, gymnastics, or soccer.

When selecting your pork shoulder—also called pork butt or Boston butt—it doesn't matter if you choose one with or without a bone. Some people will tell you it does, but it's a personal preference. However, do check the fat content. You want some fat or your pork will dry out but too much can be overly fatty, just like with ribs. The fat cap should be less than 1 inch deep.

TENDERLOINS

Pork tenderloins are among the simplest smoke preparations on the grill but they're always impressive. I smoke a couple of tenderloins for my family every couple of weeks and they never get tired of them. The pellet grill or smoker does an amazing job with tenderloins, ensuring a juicy result each time.

When selecting tenderloins, as with most pork, the key is fat content. I try to limit the fat content on my tenderloins. A pellet grill will work to keep them moist and will limit dried-out areas.

Beef

When I think smoking and barbecue, my mind immediately goes to beef: large cuts of brisket and tri-tip, steaks over a flame. Fortunately, with today's grill technology, all of these are possible on a pellet grill.

But the dream of so many pit masters is that perfect Texas-style brisket. We have all spent hours researching how best to achieve it:

Wrapped or unwrapped? Foil or butcher paper? How long should it take?

We also want steaks that even the owner of the best steakhouse would pay for—the smoke and the butter and the fire, all infused with the smell of searing meat. That's what we aim for in our backyards.

This is why I think "beef" when I think of smoking and barbecue.

Selecting beef is made easier by its grade. We'll go into this here, as well as some other tips to make you a master of low-and-slow meat cooking.

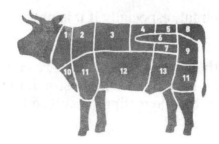

1. **Neck**	6. **Tenderloin**	11. **Shoulder Clod**
2. Chuck	7. Top Sirloin	12. Short Plate
3. **Rib**	8. **Rump Cap**	13. **Flank**
4. Short Loin	9. Round	
5. **Sirloin**	10. **Brisket**	

BRISKET

In my experience, brisket tends to be the gold standard, and among the most difficult to cook, on the pellet grill. Many look at the perfect brisket with reverence and hope for the day when they'll successfully achieve it. Discussions fill message boards on the bend test, the pull test, and the like.

The problem with this line of thinking around brisket? Well, it's not that difficult to make! Brisket, just like anything else, can be perfected with practice and patience.

When selecting the perfect brisket—and I am referring to a full brisket, with both the point and flat cuts (usually separated at most butchers) intact—the key is not too fat. If you buy a brisket with a huge fat cap, you are just going to cut it off.

Also, I suggest spending the extra money on the highest grade of brisket available to you. A cheap brisket can equal a tough brisket. Brisket is not a cheap cut anyway, so spend the money for the best cut.

TRI-TIP

If pork ribs are my number one dish, tri-tip is my number two. I have spent many weekends working to perfect my tri-tip. I have used pellet grills, charcoal Kamas's, and wood chip smokers, all in the quest to make the best tri-tip possible. Fortunately for us, my best tri-tip has come off a pellet grill.

Tri-tip is lean meat that packs amazing flavor.

When cooked properly, tri-tip can smoke as well as any meat, but with beautiful pink, juicy center.

Eating great smoked tri-tip is like eating only the best part of the best-cooked steak.

As with other meats and cuts of meat, go lean on your tri-tip. It should have good, consistent marbling (the flecks of white fat seen in each cut of meat).

RIBS

I make beef ribs significantly less often than pork, and this is by no fault of the cows. Although I enjoy beef ribs, my wife does not, and that means their beefy goodness tends to elude me.

Beef back ribs can be amazing, but they can also be a lot of work for next to nothing. Make sure you select meaty beef ribs. Many beef ribs are cut far too close to the bone, leaving little meat, only what exists between the bones.

PRIME RIB

Prime rib is one of those cuts packed with its flavor.

Every holiday season, prime rib orders fill the local butcher and we all try to replicate the flavor of the meat we had at the company party.

But again, the great thing about being a pellet grill owner is now your dish will be better than the party version. (Unfortunately, that might mean your pals will start asking you to cater!)

The grade of meat decides what rib roast you choose for prime rib. Only choose prime grade rib with a generous amount of fat, as good marbling on the meat will help keep it moist and tender.

Poultry

Poultry is a central part of our food culture and history. From the Thanksgiving turkey to chicken noodle soup for the common cold, poultry is everywhere.

Little did you know, however, that it played a large part in the spread of the pellet grill?

Think back to the first meal you had from a pellet grill. Things are changing slowly, but I would still guess 70 percent of you would say some sort of chicken.

From the development of their first grills, Traeger barbecued chicken became a way to spread the pellet grill gospel from Mount Angel, Oregon to the rest of the country.

Traeger chicken was served at local festivals, sporting events, and the supermarket. We had Traeger barbecue chicken before and after high school football games, while watching the Fourth of July show at Kennedy

High School, and later at the Oregon Garden in Silverton.

"That was all something very intentional by Randy," said Brian Traeger, former CEO of Traeger Pellet Grills, referring to his older brother. "

Randy was our head of marketing at that time. He knew how well it would do."

1.Head	**4. Tail**	**7. Breast**
2.Neck	5. Tenderloin	8. Drumstick
3. Back	**6. Wing**	**9. Thigh**

CHICKEN WINGS

If you are a classic chicken wings fan like me, mark this page and get your highlighter ready. Wings are the best. I bring wings to my tailgate parties and I cook them at home when the guys come over to watch the game. I know I am getting stereotypical, but I love wings and that is typically the time I like to enjoy them.

Wings cooked on a pellet grill or smoker are perfect for one reason: smoke. Where every bar in town has Buffalo wings or sweet and spicy wings, you now have smoky Buffalo wings and smoky-sweet and spicy wings—and smoky is just better.

TURKEY

That perfect Thanksgiving turkey will make you the holiday hero of your family. The days of oven-cooked turkey or experimenting with dangerous fryers are over. The pellet grill or smoker is perfect for making that smoky yet moist golden bird.

I take any opportunity to make turkey throughout the year. I enjoy the flavor of turkey slightly more than chicken and the pellet grill does such a good job of making it an easy process.

When selecting turkey, don't get one that is already brined. You'll make it extra salty by bringing it again or injecting it. Read the outside of the package; the ingredients will let you know if there is salt or any other solution already added.

TURKEY DRUMSTICKS

There isn't much to selecting a turkey drumstick, but if I were to make one rule, it would be to go big. Bigger is better, right?

Lamb

Lamb is the meat I had little interest in learning to cook when I was younger. The gaminess of the meat was a challenge for me to conquer and I took suggestion after suggestion, all with little or no luck in the end. Luckily for the lamb industry, my tastes have changed as I have gotten older.

Lamb greets fresh herbs with open arms. I seriously suggest having a small herb garden at home, not just for lamb, but for all your grilling. Fresh herbs take well to meat and it's hard to beat the price. Mint and rosemary are what I suggest with lamb, but thyme and basil are two herbs you must have in your garden as well.

1.Head	**6. Rib**	**11. Flank**
2.Tongue	7. Loin	12. Fore Shank
3.Cheek	**8. Sirloin**	**13. Hind Flank**
4.Neck	9. Leg	
5.Shoulder	**10. Breast**	

LAMB CHOPS

I suggest using rib chops, as they are the tenderest, but loin or shoulder chops are great, too. (Shoulder chops are so tasty.)

LEG OF LAMB

A leg of lamb can be roasted, smoky perfection. The wood-fired flame gives it that old-world taste and packs it with moist flavor.

Cooking your leg of lamb on a pellet grill or smoker will wow your friends.

Most of us are used to leg of lamb from an oven and the comparison just isn't possible. The pellet grill fills your meat with that hardwood smokiness that your oven can't touch.

When selecting your leg, try not to go too lean.

The fat in the leg, like most other meats, will work to keep the meat from drying out while roasting. Bone-in or out is a preference. Although bone-in may give slightly more flavor, it is more difficult to cut.

RACK OF LAMB

If you can find it, get an already trimmed rack of lamb to save precious prep time.

Fish

If I could, I would spend all my time cooking seafood. I love seafood. Salmon, oysters, tuna, halibut, calamari. . .

The beauty of seafood is that there is a lot of it. There is a larger variety of creatures in the vast oceans than anywhere else on the planet—land or air—and the flavor varieties are just as vast. Among my favorite flavors are the Cajun flavor of Louisiana and the Baja flavor of Southern California. Being able to travel only enhances my love of seafood; I pick up a seafood rub at every coastal destination I visit.

SALMON

The wood-fired flavor is a natural pairing with salmon. Salmon was and is a central part of the diet of indigenous people in the Pacific Northwest, who set the precedent for the processes used to smoke salmon today.

When selecting salmon, always choose wild over farmed for better flavor and because it's typically fresh, not frozen.

TUNA

Tuna is similar to most seafood. Try for fresh, if you can. Avoid anything that looks dried out or like it may have freezer burn.

SHRIMP

Shrimp is not only one of my favorite seafood, but also one of my favorite foods, period. There are so many ways to prepare shrimp that I am never let down. I have spent hours cooking shrimp on and off pellet grills, and if you know how long shrimp takes (not very long), hours of experience equal tons of shrimp.

From blackened to barbecued, there are many spectacular ways of preparing shrimp and the pellet grill only adds to the variety.

Try to find fresh, never-frozen shrimp and always choose full-size shrimp, not the little salad

OYSTERS

In the shell is how we will usually prepare oysters on the pellet grill or smoker. I aim for medium-size because they're easy to deal with and eat.

CHAPTER 8:

Useful Tips for Grill Traeger Users

To give more flavors to your meat, fish, or vegetables, consider preparing a marinade in which you leave the food for 1 or 2 hours in the refrigerator. Example of marinade: olive oil, lemon, Provence herbs.

Drain foods well before grilling them.

Salt and pepper the food at the end of cooking and not before cooking.

Do not prick food with a fork or any other object during cooking.

Adapt the cooking to the food. In the case of overcooking, do not eat the blackened parts.

Cooking times for grilling or barbecue food

Food Average Cooking Time

2-3 cm thick veal or lamb chop 9-10 minutes

Beef rib 5 cm thick 20 minutes

Skewer 7-8 minutes

Chopped steak 6-7 minutes

Whole fish of 500 g 15-20 minutes

1 kg whole fish 20-30 minutes

1 cm thick fish fillet 3-5 minutes

2 cm thick fish fillet 5-10 minutes

200 g chicken breast 8-12 minutes

Merguez, chipolata 10 minutes

For vegetables, the cooking time is very variable: from 5 minutes for the smallest and fragile to 20 minutes for the largest.

Tips and Tricks

So, now let us focus on some of the best tips and tricks you can use to become a smart chef and ace the art of using the wood pellet grill.

- Never ignore the use of upper racks. If you can place a water pan beneath the rack, it will allow for even better cooking.

- Always make it a point to choose the right pellets when using the grill. If you want to have a specific flavor, use flavored wood pellets. You also have mixed variants. Mostly, the food-grade version is a recommended choice.

- When the 40-pound bag of pellet is gone, make sure to thoroughly clean the grill. This will add to the longevity of your grill.

- You should make it a point to soak the wood chips in water before you start cooking. This greatly enhances the flavor.

- Lining the insides with aluminum foil might be a smart way to ensure your grill doesn't get too messy and it can save you hours of cleaning.

So, make full use of these tips and enjoy the benefits of wood pellet grills to become the chef at your garden parties and outdoor camping events. We are sure you would love to gorge on your cooked meals.

While the Traeger Wood Pellet Grill is easy to use, some people do have issues with it due to inexperience. The following tips will help you start on the right foot:

Store your Pellets Properly

Pellets go bad when exposed to humid environments. Wet wood pellets do not ignite when set aflame, and they may cause extensive damage to the Auger when used. Store them in a close-lid container to prevent contact with moisture.

Wrap Thermocouple with Aluminum Foil to Prevent Grease Build-up

When the thermocouple is covered in grease, it is unable to read temperatures accurately. Alternatively, you can clean the thermocouple after every use.

Cover the Grill when not in Use

The Traeger grill is an electrical appliance and is susceptible to water damage. Cover grill with weatherproof vinyl covers or keep in shades when idle.

Clean Grill Regularly

Develop a schedule for cleaning your grill to prevent damage or fire accidents.

Try out New Recipes and Utilize Every Function

There are two types of Traeger grill users; the passive users that barbeques once every three months, and the enthusiasts that discover new ways to cook with their beloved grill. Traeger Wood Pellet Grill is versatile and can cook different types of dishes, whether Reverse Seared Tri-tip or Spaghetti Squash. Try to find new and exciting ways to make your favorite dishes on the grill.

Pellet Storage

You have to be vigilant in storing your pellets, especially if you live in a humid climate. Damp or wet pellets will not lead to the best grilling experience—you won't be able to get a fire going. What's worse, damp or wet pellets will damage the auger since it won't be able to rotate and will burn out the motor.

I bought some 5-gallon pails, and my husband went on the hunt for sealing lids, since storing your pellets in an open container is counterproductive. We found that screw-on covers work best to keep moisture out, and they're convenient—you won't have to break your fingers trying to pry them open.

Temperature Readings

After using your grill a few times, you may notice that the temperature starts to fluctuate quite a bit. This is because of grease and soot build-up on the temperature probe used to regulate the temperature. An effortless way to stop this from happening is to clean the probe and cover it with foil. Consequently, cooking temperature readings will be more accurate.

Cover Your Grill

You may think a grill cover isn't necessary, but believe me, it's crucial. Your Traeger grill is an appliance and one with electronics inside to boot! If you want to ensure your pellet smoker's durability, protect it from the elements. If you can, move your grill under a rooftop after having a barbeque *and* use a grill cover. You don't want your pellet smoker to stop working suddenly due to water damage.

Cooking Temperatures, Times, and Doneness

You can download the Traeger App to gain access to thousands of recipes, get barbecue tips and tricks straight from the experts, and let you remotely monitor your cooking wherever and whenever. As a general guide, below are different temperatures and the time required for the following food items.

Fish and Seafood

Whitefish and Salmon can be grilled at 400-450° F for 5-8 minutes on each side or until flaky

Steamed lobster can be cooked at 200-225° F for 15 minutes per pound of lobster.

Scallops cook at 190° F for 1-1.5 hours

Shrimps require 400-450° F for 3-5 minutes on each side

Pork

Pork ribs may be smoked at 275° F for 3-6 hours

Pork loin cooks at 400° F until the internal temperature reaches 145-150° F

Pulled pork butt may be cooked at 225-250° F and until the internal temperature reaches 205° F

Bacon and sausages cook at 425° F for 7 minutes on each side or until cooked

Beef

Beef short ribs cook at 225-250° F for 4-6 hours until the meat easily pulls off from the bone

Beef brisket cooks at 250° F for 4 hours then covered with foil to cook for another 4 hours or more

Medium rare beef tenderloin cooks at 225-250° F for 3 hours

Beef jerky requires a low heat setting for 4-5 hours

Poultry

The whole chicken cooks at 400° F until internal temperature reaches 165° F

Chicken breast requires 400° F and 15 minutes on each side

Pheasant cooks at 200° F for 2-3 hours until internal temperature reaches 160° F

Smoked turkey requires a temperature of 180-225° F for 10-12 hours or until the internal temperature is 165° F the air fryer is a cooking device that was invented in 2010. It is a small countertop kitchen appliance that looks like a convection oven. It cooks food using the process of hot air circulation with the use of a mechanical fan.

CHAPTER 9:

Different Types of Cooking

There are five methods of cooking with the grill; they include:

- Indirect grilling

- Direct grilling

- Smoking

- Roasting

Despite fierce competition, Traeger grills continue to be the world's No 1 best-selling wood pellet grill because of its mastery of the wood-fired cooking craft. The grill is capable of transforming a simple fare into an extraordinary dish with its wood-fired flavoring. The grill temperatures can range from 150°F to well over 375°F to enable it to grill, sear, roast, smoke, and bake. It produces consistent results.

Components of Wood Pellet Grill and their Functions

There are five models of Traeger Pellet Grills available, depending on the size and capabilities. The models include:

- Pro Series

- Ironwood Series

- Timberline Series

- Portable Grill Series

Commercial Grill Series Some of the components featured in the models are:

Pellet Hopper: This is the part of the grill that stores the wood pellets. It's recommended to keep it filled to prevent interruption of cooking activities. The number of pellets used depends on the time and temperature required for cooking a particular meal.

Porcelain-Coated Grill Grate: This holds the food to be prepared. It is coated with porcelain to prevent the sticking of meals. The grate is also very easy to clean.

Cast Iron Grate: This grate allows for even distribution of heat when grilling. It creates a perfect sear when used.

Steel Construction: Made from cold-rolled steels, they are durable and reliable as a cover for the Traeger grill. It helps with the regulation of temperature and can be cleaned easily because of its non-stick surface.

Convection Blower: This is important to the grill as it is responsible for maintaining a constant flow of air to keep the pellets in the Firepot aflame.

Auger: This conveys the pellets from the hopper to the Firepot.

AutoStart Firepot: This is where the wood pellets are ignited for cooking. It is controlled by the Thermostat and does not require any external firing methods.

Hot Rod Ignitor: When turned on, it causes the pellets in the Firepot to ignite and rise to the temperature selected on the Thermostat Controller.

Fire Baffle Plate: It is positioned around the Firepot and serves as a deflector shield to retain heat. The plate ensures that the heat produced is absorbed and spread evenly to the cooking grates.

Thermostat Controller: This is used to set the temperature of the wood pellet grill. It controls the Hot Rod Ignitor and ensures that the selected temperature is maintained throughout cooking.

Grease Drain Pan and Bucket: Used during indirect grilling, baking, roasting, and smoking. The Grease Drain Pan collects the grease produced during cooking and transports it to the Grease Bucket through the Grease Drain Tube.

Smoke Exhaust: This is used to control the flow of air out of the grill. It is essential for maintaining the temperature of the cooking chamber.

CHAPTER 10:

How to Properly Clean the Traeger Grill and Maintenance

I t is very important to know how to correctly maintain and clean your Traeger grill. You made the great choice of buying a grill that will last a lifetime, so why don't ensure that it runs smoothly for years?

To care for your Traeger grills, you have to know its main components. Even if you are not a DIY expert, and you are most likely to call a repair service, if you have a problem, you still need to know how your grill is built, even just for cleaning it properly.

There are eight main components of the machine which work together to provide you with results that you won't have with any other grill.

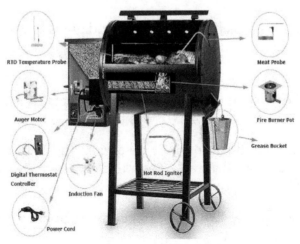

The main components are listed below:

Hardwood Pallets

These are the most important part of the grill. They function as the main fuel for the grill to work. All-natural hardwood flavorings can seep into your food while cooking through them. You can put any type of wood you want to bring a distinct taste to your dish.

Hopper

This is where you will put your wood pellets in. The flavoring happens here as the wood ignites and cooks the food. 100% wood with no charcoal or gas connection required.

Controller

The knob enables you to set the temperature of your choice and regulate it during the cooking process.

Induction Fan

The fan turns on as you turn on the grill and heat the food evenly by using the convection process for cooking. The Fan transfers hot air to the entirety of the grill, making it evenly distributed.

Auger

It is a screw-like device that picks and places the wood pellets into the firepot to start the ignition process.

Hot Rod

This is where the pellets meet the fire and fire catches on. It is at the end of the auger.

Firepot

Automatically fire is turned on, which ignites the hotrod and causes pellets to catch fire.

Drip Tray

This piece of metal just above the fire prevents it from directly reaching the grill and reduces charring on food. It allows heat and smoke to pass through.

Making sure your grill is clean and free of built-up grease and debris is critical for keeping the pure, woodfired flavor of your grill intact. The best way to ensure this is through regular cleanings and maintenance of your grill.

NOTE: Make sure that your grill is switched off and not connected to the electrical outlet!

You'll want the following items on hand:

• Wooden Grill Grate Scrape

• Grease Cleaner. Trager markets a Traeger All-Natural Grease Cleaner, but your normal kitchen grease cleaner will work just as well. Even better, if you clean it frequently, you might want to consider using vinegar or lemon juice diluted with water (at 60%) in a spray bottle.

• Drip Tray Liners

• Bucket Liners

• Shop Vac

• Paper Towels

• Bottle Brush

• Disposable Gloves

Step 1 Spray grates with the grease cleaner

Step 2 Spray inside of the chimney

Step 3 Remove and clean grates with the Wooden Grill Grate Scrape. Don't use wire brushes and wipe the grates down with a cleaning cloth or heavy-duty paper towels for this.

Step 4 Remove drip tray liner

Step 5 Remove the drip tray

Step 6 Remove heat baffle

Step 7 Vacuum inside of the grill.

Step 8 Scrub inside of the chimney with a bottle brush. Again, don't use wire brushes and wipe the grates down with a cleaning cloth or heavy-duty paper towels for this.

Step 9 Spray walls with your grease cleaner

Step 10 Let soak and wipe down with paper towels

Step 11 Reinsert heat baffle

Step 12 Reinsert drip tray

Step 13 Insert new drip tray liner

Step 14 Insert new bucket liner

Step 15 Reinsert grates

You don't have to go through the whole process every time you grill; after all the meat takes its flavor also from the charred and impregnated grates from all the previous barbecues. But you should do it twice, or three times per grilling season, if you use it frequently. If you are cooking something particularly greasy, we would recommend that you clean it right after. It will make the job a lot easier if you don't let the fat congeal.

To avoid problems and making the cleaning process a bit easier, here are some helpful tips for routine maintenance:

Invest in a cover. The Traeger covers are a bit expensive but aesthetically pleasing. If you don't want to buy a Trager cover, then make sure to cover it carefully with a plastic sheet. If your Traeger grill is stored outside during wet weather, you risk that water gets into the hopper. When the pellets get wet, they expand and may clog your auger. Also, you cannot cook with wet wood.

Change the foil on your grease pan often, and clean underneath the foil as well. Grease is easier to clean when it is still a bit warm; so after you have finished barbecuing, even if you are tempted to sleep off the party, take the time to scrape the extra grease and debris from the greased pan and grease drain tube and replace the grease pan foil, to avoid grease build-up. If the drain tube gets clogged, you may risk a grease fire.

Empty the grease bucket. Yuck, I know! But it is a simple enough job: empty the grease in something you can discard, such as a plastic bottle; don't pour it down the drain or in the gutter! Clean the bucket with hot water and soap or, to make your job easier, line the bucket with aluminum foil that you can simply discard.

Wipe down the exterior surfaces. The Trager grills are beautiful objects, so keep the powder coating looking new! Use warm water and soap and wipe it with a clean cloth or paper towels. Don't use abrasive cleaners or scouring pads!

Remove extra ash from the fire pot, even if you don't want to clean it completely, at least once every 5 times you use it, remove the grates, the drain pan, and the heat baffle to remove the ash in and around the firepot. You can use a shop vac for this job. Make sure that all the components are cold and the grill is unplugged and not switched on.

CHAPTER 11:

Breakfast

Breakfast Sausage

Preparation Time: 60 minutes

Cooking Time: 9 hours

Servings: 6

Ingredients:

20/22-millimeter natural sheep casings, rinsed

Warm water

2 lb. ground pork

Apple butter rub

Pinch dried marjoram

1/2 teaspoon ground cloves

1 tablespoon brown sugar

1/3 cup ice water

Pepper to taste

Directions:

Soak the sheep casings in warm water for 1 hour.

In a bowl, mix all the ingredients.

Use a mixer set on low speed to combine the ingredients.

Cover and refrigerate the mixture for 15 minutes.

Insert the casings into the sausage stuffer.

Stuff the casings with the ground pork mixture.

Twist into five links.

Remove bubbles using a picker.

Put the sausages on a baking pan.

Refrigerate for 24 hours.

Set your wood pellet grill to smoke.

Hang the sausages on hooks and put them in the smoking cabinet.

Set the temperature to 350 degrees F.

Smoke the sausages for 1 hour.

Increase the temperature to 425 degrees F.

Cook for another 30 minutes.

Nutrition:

Calories: 220

Fat: 19 g

Cholesterol: 45 mg

Carbohydrates: 1 g

Fiber: 0 g

Sugars: 1 g

Protein: 11 g

Corned Beef Hash

Preparation Time: 30 minutes

Cooking Time: 4 hours

Servings: 4

Ingredients:

2 lb. corned beef brisket

Pepper to taste

2 cups chicken broth

1 lb. potatoes, peeled

6 slices bacon, chopped

1 red bell pepper, chopped

1 onion, chopped

1 teaspoon thyme, chopped

1-1/2 teaspoon hickory bacon rub

2 tablespoons parsley, chopped

Directions:

Season the corned beef with the seasoning packet from its package and with the pepper.

Let it rest for 30 minutes.

Set your wood pellet grill to smoke for 10 to 15 minutes.

Set it to 225 degrees F.

Place the corned beef on top of the grills.

Smoke for 3 hours.

Transfer the corned beef to a baking pan.

Add the chicken broth and potatoes to the pan.

Cover the pan with foil.

Cook for 30 minutes.

Let the corned beef and potatoes cool.

Refrigerate for 1 hour.

Slice the potatoes and corned beef.

Add a cast-iron pan to the pellet grill.

Preheat it to 400 degrees F.

Cook the bacon until golden and crispy.

Transfer to a plate lined with a paper towel.

Add the red bell pepper and onion to the pan.

Cook for 3 minutes.

Stir in the corned beef.

Add the rest of the ingredients.

Serve while hot.

Nutrition:

Calories: 380

Fat: 24 g

Cholesterol: 80mg

Carbohydrates: 22.1 g

Fiber: 1.9 g

Sugars: 1.1 g

Protein: 20

Turkey Sandwich

Preparation Time: 10 minutes

Cooking Time: 20 minutes

Servings: 4

Ingredients:

8 bread slices

1 cup gravy

2 cups turkey, cooked and shredded

Directions:

Set your wood pellet grill to smoke.

Preheat it to 400 degrees F.

Place a grill mat on top of the grates.

Add the turkey on top of the mat.

Cook for 10 minutes.

Toast the bread in the flame broiler.

Top the bread with the gravy and shredded turkey.

Nutrition:

Calories: 280

Fat: 3.5 g

Cholesterol: 20 mg

Carbohydrates: 46 g

Fiber: 5 g

Sugars: 7 g

Protein: 18 g

Scrambled Eggs

Preparation Time: 5 Minutes

Cooking Time: 10 Minutes

Servings: 3 to 4

Ingredients:

1/4 cup Cheddar and Monterey Cheese Blend, shredded

Sea Salt and Black Pepper, as needed

1 tbsp. Butter

6 Eggs

3 tbsp. Nut Milk or milk of your choice

Green onion or fresh herbs of your choice, for garnish

Directions:

First, place eggs, milk, cheese blend, pepper, and salt in the blender pitcher.

Next, press the 'medium' button and blend the mixture for 25 to 30 seconds or until everything comes together and is frothy.

Then, heat the butter in a medium-sized saucepan over medium-low heat.

Once the skillet becomes hot and the butter has melted, swirl the pan so that the butter coats all the sides. Pour the egg mixture into it and allow it to sit for 20 seconds. With a spatula, break it down and continue cooking until the egg is set and cooked. Garnish with green onion. Serve it along with toasted bread.

Nutrition:

Calories: 70

Fat: 5.6 g

Total Carbs: 0.3 g

Fiber: 0 g

Sugar: 0.3 g

Protein: 4.7 g

Cholesterol: 157.5 mg

Berry Smoothie

Preparation Time: 5 Minutes

Cooking Time: 1 Minute

Servings: 1

Ingredients:

2 scoops Protein Powder

2 cups Almond Milk

4 cups Mixed Berry

2 cups Yoghurt

Directions:

First, place mixed berry, protein powder, yogurt, and almond milk in the blender pitcher. Then, select the 'smoothie' button. Finally, pour the smoothie into the serving glass.

Nutrition:

Calories: 112

Fat: 2 g

Total Carbs: 26 g

Fiber: 0 g

Sugar: 0 g

Protein: 1 g

Cholesterol: 0

Avocado Smoothie

Preparation Time: 5 Minutes

Cooking Time: 5 Minutes

Servings: 2

Ingredients:

1 cup Coconut Milk, preferably full-fat

1 cup Ice

3 cups Baby Spinach

1 Banana, frozen and quartered

1/2 cup pineapple chunks, frozen

1/2 of 1 Avocado, smooth

Directions:

First, place ice, pineapple chunks, pineapple chunks, banana, avocado, baby spinach in the blender pitcher.

Now, press the 'extract' button.

Finally, transfer to a serving glass.

Nutrition:

Fat: 25.1 g

Calories: 323

Total Carbs: 29.2 g

Fiber: 11.4 g

Sugar: 8.3 g

Protein: 5.1 g

Cholesterol: 0

Tofu Smoothie

Preparation Time: 5 Minutes

Cooking Time: 5 Minutes

Servings: 2

Ingredients:

1 Banana, sliced and frozen

3/4 cup Almond Milk

2 tbsp. Peanut Butter

1/2 cup Yoghurt, plain and low-fat

1/2 cup Tofu, soft and silken

1/3 cup Dates, chopped

Directions:

First, place tofu, banana, dates, yogurt, peanut butter, and almond milk in the blender pitcher.

After that, press the 'smoothie' button.

Finally, transfer to the serving glass and enjoy it.

Nutrition:

Fat: 0 g

Calories: 330

Total Carbs: 0 g

Fiber: 0 g

Sugar: 0 g

Protein: 0 g

Cholesterol: 0

Banana Nut Oatmeal

Preparation Time: 5 Minutes

Cooking Time: 5 Minutes

Servings: 2

Ingredients:

1/2 tbsp. Maple Syrup

1/4 cup Hemp Seeds

1/2 cup Steel Cut Oats

Dash of Sea Salt

1 tsp. Vanilla Extract

1/2 cup Water

1/2 tsp. Cinnamon

1 tsp. Nutmeg

1/3 cup Milk

1 Banana, medium, sliced and divided

Directions:

First, keep half of the banana, salt, oats, vanilla, cinnamon, almond milk, nutmeg, and maple syrup in the blender pitcher.

After that, press the 'cook' button and then the 'high' button.

Cook for 5 minutes.

Once done, divide the oatmeal among the serving bowls and top it with the remaining sliced banana and hemp seeds.

Nutrition:

Fat: 5.3 g

Calories: 189

Total Carbs: 34.9 g

Fiber: 7.5 g

Sugar: 15.3 g

Protein: 3.9 g

Cholesterol: 0

Carrot Strawberry Smoothie

Preparation Time: 5 Minutes

Cooking Time: 5 Minutes

Servings: 2

Ingredients:

1/3 cup Bell Pepper, diced

1 cup Carrot Juice, chilled

1 cup mango, diced

1 cup Strawberries, unsweetened and frozen

Directions:

To start with, place strawberries, bell pepper, and mango in the blender pitcher.

After that, pulse it a few times.

Next, pour the carrot juice into it.

Finally, press the 'smoothie' button.

Nutrition:

Fat: 5.5 g

Calories: 334

Total Carbs: 61 g

Fiber: 12.7 g

Sugar: 34 g

Protein: 10.4 g

Cholesterol: 7.5 mg

Green Smoothie

Preparation Time: 5 Minutes

Cooking Time: 5 Minutes

Servings: 3 to 4

Ingredients:

1/4 cup Baby Spinach

1/2 cup Ice

1/4 cup Kale

1/2 cup Pineapple Chunks

1/2 cup Coconut Water

1/2 cup mango, diced

1/2 banana, diced

Directions:

Begin by placing all the ingredients needed to make the smoothie in the blender pitcher.

Now, press the 'extract' button.

Transfer the smoothie into the serving glass.

Nutrition:

Calories: 184

Fat: 1.3 g

Total Carbs: 44.6 g

Fiber: 4.5 g

Sugar: 21.9 g

Protein: 4.3 g

Choleterol: 0

Kid-friendly Zucchini Bread

Preparation Time: 15 minutes

Cooking Time: 50 minutes

Servings: 4

Ingredients:

1 ½ cup whole wheat flour

2 eggs

1 tsp salt

1 tsp baking powder

1 tsp baking soda

½ cup maple syrup

4 tbsp butter (melted)

2 tsp cinnamon

2 tsp vanilla extract

1 ½ cups shredded zucchini

2 tbsp lemon juice

1 tsp ground nutmeg

Directions:

Start your grill on smoke mode, leave the lip open for 5 minutes, or until the fire starts.

Close the lid and preheat the grill to 350°F for 15 minutes, using apple hardwood pellets.

Wrap the shredded zucchini with a clean kitchen towel and squeeze to remove excess liquid. Set aside.

In a mixing bowl, whisk together the eggs, maple syrup, butter, vanilla extract, and lemon juice.

Pour the egg mixture into the flour mixture and mix until the ingredients are well combined.

Fold in the shredded zucchini.

Pour the batter into the prepared loaf pan and spread it to the edges of the pan.

Place the loaf pan directly on the grill and bake until a toothpick inserted in the middle of the bread comes out clean.

Remove the loaf pan from the grill and transfer the bread to a wire rack to cool.

Serve and enjoy.

Nutrition:

Calories: 428

Total Fat: 14.6 g

Saturated Fat: 8.3 g

Cholesterol: 112 mg

Sodium: 1020 mg

Total Carbohydrate 66 g

Dietary Fiber 2.5 g

Total Sugars: 25.1 g

Protein: 8.4 g

Breakfast Sausage Casserole

Preparation Time: 15 minutes

Cooking Time: 30 minutes

Servings: 6

Ingredients:

1-pound ground sausage

1 tsp ground sage

¼ cup green beans (chopped)

2 tsp yellow mustard

1 tsp cayenne

8 tbsp mayonnaise

1 large onion (diced)

2 cups diced zucchini

2 cups shredded cabbage

1 ½ cup shredded cheddar cheese

Chopped fresh parsley to taste

Directions:

Preheat the grill to 360°F and grease a cast-iron casserole dish.

Heat a large skillet over medium to high heat.

Toss the sausage into the skillet, break it apart and cook until browned, stirring constantly.

Add the cabbage, zucchini, green beans, and onion and cook until the vegetables are tender, stirring frequently.

Pour the cooked sausage and vegetable into the casserole dish and spread it.

Break the eggs into a mixing bowl and add the mustard, cayenne, mayonnaise, and sage. Whish until well combined.

Stir in half of the cheddar cheese.

Pour the egg mixture over the ingredients in the casserole dish.

Sprinkle with the remaining shredded cheese.

Place the baking dish on the grill and bake until the top of the casserole turns golden brown.

Garnish with chopped fresh parsley.

Nutrition:

Calories: 472

Total Fat: 37.6 g

Saturated Fat: 13.9 g

Cholesterol: 98 mg

Sodium: 909 mg

Total Carbohydrate 10.7 g

Dietary Fiber 1.9 g

Total Sugars: 4 g

Protein: 23.1 g

Keto Quiche

Preparation Time: 10 minutes

Cooking Time: 45 minutes

Servings: 6

Ingredients:

12 tbsp unsalted butter (soften)

12 large eggs

8 ounces grated cheddar cheese (divided)

4 ounces cream cheese

½ tsp salt or to taste

½ tsp ground black pepper or to taste

1 yellow onion (diced)

1 green bell pepper (chopped)

3 cups broccoli florets (chopped)

1 tbsp olive oil

Directions:

Preheat the grill to 325°F with the lid closed for 15 minutes.

Heat the olive oil in a skillet over high heat.

Add the chopped onion, broccoli, and green pepper. Cook for about 8 minutes, stirring constantly.

Remove the skillet from heat.

Process the egg and cheese in a food processor, adding the melted butter in a bit while processing.

Combine 4ounce grated cheddar cheese, salt, and pepper in a quiche pan.

Toss the cooked vegetable into the pan and mix.

Pour the egg mixture over the ingredients in the quiche pan.

Sprinkle the remaining grated cheese over it.

Place the pan in the preheated grill and bake for 45 minutes.

Remove and transfer the quiche to a rack to cool.

Slice and serve.

Nutrition:

Calories: 615

Total Fat: 54.7 g

Saturated Fat: 30.1 g

Cholesterol: 494 mg

Sodium: 804 mg

Total Carbohydrate 8.1 g

Dietary Fiber 1.9 g

Total Sugars: 3.6 g

Protein: 25.4 g

CHAPTER 12:

Beef Recipes

Smoked and Pulled Beef

Preparation Time: 10 minutes

Cooking Time: 6 hours

Servings: 6

Ingredients:

4 lb. beef sirloin tip roast

1/2 cup BBQ rub

2 bottles of amber beer

1 bottle barbecues sauce

Directions:

Turn your wood pellet grill on smoke setting then trim excess fat from the steak.

Coat the steak with BBQ rub and let it smoke on the grill for 1 hour.

Continue cooking and flipping the steak for the next 3 hours. Transfer the steak to a braising vessel. Add the beers.

Braise the beef until tender then transfer to a platter reserving 2 cups of cooking liquid.

Use a pair of forks to shred the beef and return it to the pan. Add the reserved liquid and barbecue sauce. Stir well and keep warm before serving.

Enjoy.

Nutrition:

Calories 829,

Total fat 46g,

Saturated fat 18g,

Total carbs 4g,

Net carbs 4g,

Protein 86g,

Sugar 0g,

Fiber 0g,

Sodium: 181mg

Wood Pellet Smoked Beef Jerky

Preparation Time: 15 minutes

Cooking Time: 5 hours

Servings: 10

Ingredients:

3 lb sirloin steaks, sliced into 1/4-inch thickness

2 cups soy sauce

1/2 cup brown sugar

1 cup pineapple juice

2 tbsp sriracha

2 tbsp red pepper flake

2 tbsp hoisin

2 tbsp onion powder

2 tbsp rice wine vinegar

2 tbsp garlic, minced

Directions:

Mix all the ingredients in a zip lock-bag. Seal the bag and mix until the beef is well coated. Ensure you get as much air as possible from the zip-lock bag.

Put the bag in the fridge overnight to let marinate. Remove the bag from the fridge 1 hour before cooking.

Start your wood pallet grill and set it to smoke. Layout the meat on the grill with half-inch space between them.

Let them cook for 5 hours while turning after every 2-1/2 hours.

Transfer from the grill and let cool for 30 minutes before serving.

enjoy.

Nutrition:

Calories 80,

Total fat 1g,

Saturated fat 0g,

Total carbs 5g,

 Net carbs 5g,

Protein 14g,

Sugar 5g,

Fiber 0g,

Sodium: 650mg

Reverse Seared Flank Steak

Preparation Time: 10 minutes

Cooking Time: 10 minutes

Servings: 2

Ingredients:

1.5 lb Flanks steak

1 tbsp salt

1/2 onion powder

1/4 tbsp garlic powder

1/2 black pepper, coarsely ground

Directions:

Preheat your wood pellet grill to 225f

In a mixing bowl, mix salt, onion powder, garlic powder, and pepper. Generously rub the steak with the mixture.

Place the steaks on the preheated grill, close the lid, and let the steak cook.

Crank up the grill to high then let it heat. The steak should be off the grill and tented with foil to keep it warm.

Once the grill is heated up to 450°F, place the steak back and grill for 3 minutes per side.

Remove from heat, pat with butter, and serve. Enjoy.

Nutrition:

Calories 112,

Total fat 5g,

Saturated fat 2g,

Total carbs 1g,

Net carbs 1g,

Protein 16g,

Sugar 0g,

Fiber 0g,

Sodium: 737mg

Smoked Midnight Brisket

Preparation Time: 15 minutes

Cooking Time: 12 hours

Servings: 6

Ingredients:

1 tbsp Worcestershire sauce

1 tbsp Traeger beef Rub

1 tbsp Traeger Chicken rub

1 tbsp Traeger Blackened Saskatchewan rub

5 lb. flat cut brisket

1 cup beef broth

Directions:

Rub the sauce and rubs in a mixing bowl then rub the mixture on the meat.

Preheat your grill to 180°F with the lid closed for 15 minutes. You can use super smoke if you desire.

Place the meat on the grill and grill for 6 hours or until the internal temperature reaches 160°F.

Remove the meat from the grill and double wrap it with foil.

Add beef broth and return to grill with the temperature increased to 225°F. Cook for 4 hours or until the internal temperature reaches 204°F.

Remove from the grill and let rest for 30 minutes. Serve and enjoy with your favorite BBQ sauce.

Nutrition:

Calories 200,

Total fat 14g,

Saturated fat 6g,

Total carbs 3g,

Net carbs 3g,

Protein 14g,

Sugar 0g,

Fiber 0g,

Sodium: 680mg

Grilled Butter Basted Porterhouse Steak

Preparation Time: 10 minutes

Cooking Time: 40 minutes

Servings: 4

Ingredients:

4 tbsp butter, melted

2 tbsp Worcestershire sauce

2 tbsp Dijon mustard

Traeger Prime rib rub

Directions:

Set your wood pellet grill to 225°F with the lid closed for 15 minutes.

In a mixing bowl, mix butter, sauce, Dijon mustard until smooth. brush the mixture on the meat then season with the rub.

Arrange the meat on the grill grate and cook for 30 minutes.

Use tongs to transfer the meat to a pattern then increase the heat to high.

Return the meat to the grill grate to grill until your desired doneness is achieved.

Baste with the butter mixture again if you desire and let rest for 3 minutes before serving. Enjoy.

Nutrition:

Calories 726,

Total fat 62g,

Saturated fat 37g,

Total carbs 5g,

Net carbs 4g,

Protein 36g,

Sugar 1g,

Fiber 1g,

Sodium: 97mg,

Potassium 608mg

Cocoa Crusted Grilled Flank steak

Preparation Time: 10 minutes

Cooking Time: 6 minutes

Servings: 6

Ingredients:

1 tbsp cocoa powder

2 tbsp chili powder

1 tbsp chipotle chili powder

1/2 tbsp garlic powder

1/2 tbsp onion powder

1-1/2 tbsp brown sugar

1 tbsp cumin

1 tbsp smoked paprika

1 tbsp kosher salt

1/2 tbsp black pepper

Olive oil

4 lb. Flank steak

Directions:

Whisk together cocoa, chili powder, garlic powder, onion powder, sugar, cumin, paprika, salt, and pepper in a mixing bowl.

Drizzle the steak with oil then rub with the cocoa mixture on both sides.

Preheat your wood pellet grill for 15 minutes with the lid closed.

Cook the meat on the grill grate for 5 minutes or until the internal temperature reaches 135°F.

Remove the meat from the grill and let it cool for 15 minutes to allow the juices to redistribute.

Slice the meat against the grain and on a sharp diagonal.

Serve and enjoy.

Nutrition:

Calories 420,

Total fat 26g,

Saturated fat 8g,

Total carbs 21g,

Net carbs 13g,

Protein 3g,

Sugar 7g,

Fiber 8g,

Sodium: 2410mg

Wood Pellet Grill Prime Rib Roast

Preparation Time: 10 minutes

Cooking Time: 4 hours

Servings: 10

Ingredients:

7 lb. bone prime rib roast

Traeger prime rib rub

Directions:

Coat the roast generously with the rub then wrap in a plastic wrap. let sit in the fridge for 24 hours to marinate.

Set the temperatures to 500°F.to to preheat with the lid closed for 15 minutes.

Place the rib directly on the grill fat side up and cook for 30 minutes.

Reduce the temperature to 300°F and cook for 4 hours or until the internal temperature is 120°F-rare, 130°F-medium rare, 140°F-medium, and 150°F-well done.

Remove from the grill and let rest for 30 minutes then serve and enjoy.

Nutrition:

Calories 290,

Total fat 23g,

Saturated fat 9.3g,

Protein 19g,

Sodium: 54mg,

Potassium 275mg

Smoked Longhorn Cowboy Tri-Tip

Preparation Time: 10 minutes

Cooking Time: 4 hours

Servings: 7

Ingredients:

3 lb tri-tip roast 1/8 cup coffee, ground

1/4 cup Traeger beef rub

Directions:

Preheat the grill to 180°F with the lid closed for 15 minutes. Meanwhile, rub the roast with coffee and beef rub. Place the roast on the grill grate and smoke for 3 hours. Remove the roast from the grill and double wrap it with foil. Increase the temperature to 275°F. Return the meat to the grill and let cook for 90 minutes or until the internal temperature reaches 135°F.

Remove from the grill, unwrap it and let rest for 10 minutes before serving.

Nutrition:

Calories 245,

Total fat 14g,

Saturated fat 4g,

Protein 23g,

Sodium: 80mg

Wood Pellet Grill Teriyaki Beef Jerky

Preparation Time: 10 minutes

Cooking Time: 5 hours

Servings: 6

Ingredients:

3 cups soy sauce

2 cups brown sugar

3 garlic cloves

2-inch ginger knob, peeled and chopped

1 tbsp sesame oil

4 lb. beef, skirt steak

Directions:

Place all the ingredients except the meat in a food processor. Pulse until well mixed.

Trim any excess fat from the meat and slice into 1/4-inch slices. Add the steak with the marinade into a zip lock bag and let marinate for 12-24 hours in a fridge.

Set the wood pellet grill to smoke and let preheat for 5 minutes.

Arrange the steaks on the grill leaving a space between each. Let smoke for 5 hours.

Remove the steak from the grill and serve when warm.

Nutrition:

Calories 80,

Total fat 1g,

Saturated fat 0g,

Total Carbs 7g,

Net Carbs 0g,

Protein 11g,

Sugar 6g,

Fiber 0g,

Sodium: 390mg

Grilled Butter Basted Rib-eye

Preparation Time: 20 minutes

Cooking Time: 25 minutes

Servings: 4

Ingredients:

2 rib-eye steaks, bone-in

Salt to taste

Pepper to taste

4 tbsp butter, unsalted

Directions:

Mix steak, salt, and pepper in a zip-lock bag. Seal the bag and mix until the beef is well coated. Ensure you get as much air as possible from the zip-lock bag.

Set the wood pellet grill temperature to high with the lid closed for 15 minutes. Place a cast-iron into the grill.

Place the steaks on the hottest spot of the grill and cook for 5 minutes with the lid closed.

Open the lid and add butter to the skillet. When it's almost melted place the steak on the skillet with the grilled side up.

Cook for 5 minutes while busting the meat with butter. Close the lid and cook until the internal temperature is 130°F.

Remove the steak from the skillet and let rest for 10 minutes before enjoying with the reserved butter.

Nutrition:

Calories 745,

Total fat 65g,

Saturated fat 32g,

Total Carbs 5g,

Net Carbs 5g,

Protein 35g,

Wood Pellet Smoked Brisket

Preparation Time: 20 minutes

Cooking Time: 9 hours

Servings: 10

Ingredients:

2 tbsp garlic powder

2 tbsp onion powder

2 tbsp paprika

2 tbsp chili powder

1/3 cup salt

1/3 cup black pepper

12 lb whole packer brisket, trimmed

1-1/2 cup beef broth

Directions:

Set your wood pellet temperature to 225°F. Let preheat for 15 minutes with the lid closed.

Meanwhile, mix garlic, onion, paprika, chili, salt, and pepper in a mixing bowl.

Season the brisket generously on all sides.

Place the meat on the grill with the fat side down and let it cool until the internal temperature reaches 160°F. Remove the meat from the grill and double wrap it with foil. Return it to the grill and cook until the internal temperature reaches 204°F.

Remove from the grill, unwrap the brisket, and let sit for 15 minutes.

Slice and serve.

Nutrition:

Calories 270,

Total fat 20g,

Saturated fat 8g,

Total Carbs 3g,

Net Carbs 3g,

Protein 20g,

Sugar 1g,

Fiber 0g,

Sodium: 1220mg

Traeger Beef Jerky

Preparation Time: 15 minutes

Cooking Time: 5 hours

Servings: 10

Ingredients:

3 lb. sirloin steaks

2 cups soy sauce

1 cup pineapple juice

1/2 cup brown sugar

2 tbsp sriracha

2 tbsp hoisin

2 tbsp red pepper flake

2 tbsp rice wine vinegar

2 tbsp onion powder

Directions:

Mix the marinade in a zip lock bag and add the beef. Mix until well coated and remove as much air as possible.

Place the bag in a fridge and let marinate overnight or for 6 hours. Remove the bag from the fridge an hour before cooking 3) Startup the Traeger and set it on the smoking settings or at 190ºF.

Lay the meat on the grill leaving a half-inch space between the pieces. Let cool for 5 hours and turn after 2 hours.

Remove from the grill and let cool. Serve or refrigerate

Nutrition:

Calories 309,

Total fat 7g,

Saturated fat 3g,

Total carbs 20g,

Net carbs 19g

Protein 34g,

Sugars 15g,

Fiber 1g,

Sodium 2832mg

Traeger Smoked Beef Roast

Preparation Time: 10 minutes

Cooking Time: 6 hours

Servings: 6

Ingredients:

1-3/4 lb. beef sirloin tip roast

1/2 cup BBQ rub

2 bottles of amber beer

1 bottle BBQ sauce

Directions:

Turn the Traeger onto the smoke setting.

Transfer the beef to a pan and add the beer. The beef should be 1/2 way covered.

Braise the beef until fork tender. It will take 3 hours on the stovetop and 60 minutes on the instant pot.

Remove the beef from the ban and reserve 1 cup of the cooking liquid.

Use 2 forks to shred the beef into small pieces then return to the pan with the reserved braising liquid.

Add BBQ sauce and stir well then keep warm until serving. You can also reheat if it gets cold.

Nutrition:

Calories 829,

Total fat 46g,

Saturated fat 18g,

Total carbs 4g,

Net carbs 4g

Protein 86g,

Sugars 0g,

Fiber 0g,

Sodium 181mmg

Reverse Seared Flank Steak

Preparation Time: 10 minutes

Cooking Time: 20 minutes

Servings: 2

Ingredients:

3 lb. flank steaks

1 tbsp salt

1/2 tbsp onion powder

1/4 tbsp garlic powder

1/2 black pepper, coarsely ground

Directions:

Preheat the Traeger to $225°F$.

All the ingredients in a bowl and mix well. Add the steaks and rub them generously with the rub mixture. Place the steak on the grill and close the lid. Let cook until its internal temperature is $10°F$ under your desired temperature. $115°F$ for rare, $125°F$ for the medium rear, and $135°F$ for medium. Wrap the steak with foil and raise the grill temperature to high. Place back the steak and grill for 3 minutes on each side. Pat with butter and serve when hot.

Nutrition:

Calories 112, Total fat 5g,

Saturated fat 2g, Total carbs 1g,

Net carbs 1g Protein 16g, Sodium 737mg

Traeger Beef Tenderloin

Preparation Time: 10 minutes

Cooking Time: 45 minutes

Servings: 6

Ingredients:

4 lb. beef tenderloin

3 tbsp steak rub

1 tbsp kosher salt

Directions:

Preheat the Traeger to high heat. Meanwhile, trim excess fat from the beef and cut it into 3 pieces. Coat the steak with rub and kosher salt. Place it on the grill. Close the lid and cook for 10 minutes. Open the lid, flip the beef and cook for 10 more minutes. Reduce the temperature of the grill to 225_0F and smoke the beef until the internal temperature reaches 130_0F.

Remove the beef from the grill and let rest for 15 minutes before slicing and serving.

Nutrition:

Calories 999,

Total fat 76g,

Saturated fat 30g,

Protein 74g,

Sodium 1234mmg

Trager New York Strip

Preparation Time: 5 minutes

Cooking Time: 15 minutes

Servings: 6

Ingredients:

3 New York strips

Salt and pepper

Directions:

If the steak is in the fridge, remove it 30 minutes before cooking.

Preheat the Traeger to 450_0F.

Meanwhile, season the steak generously with salt and pepper. Place it on the grill and let it cook for 5 minutes per side or until the internal temperature reaches 128_0F.

Remove the steak from the grill and let it rest for 10 minutes.

Nutrition:

Calories 198,

Total fat 14g,

Saturated fat 6g,

Protein 17g,

Sodium 115mg

Traeger Stuffed Peppers

Preparation Time: 20 minutes

Cooking Time: 5 minutes

Servings: 6

Ingredients:

3 bell peppers, sliced in halves

1 lb. ground beef, lean

1 onion, chopped

1/2 tbsp red pepper flakes

1/2 tbsp salt

1/4 tbsp pepper

1/2 tbsp garlic powder

1/2 tbsp onion powder

1/2 cup white rice

15 oz stewed tomatoes

8 oz tomato sauce

6 cups cabbage, shredded

1-1/2 cup water

2 cups cheddar cheese

Directions:

Arrange the pepper halves on a baking tray and set aside.

Preheat your grill to $325{\circ}F$.

Brown the meat in a large skillet. Add onions, pepper flakes, salt, pepper garlic, and onion and cook until the meat is well cooked.

Add rice, stewed tomatoes, tomato sauce, cabbage, and water.

Cover and simmer until the rice is well cooked, the cabbage is tender and there is no water in the rice.

Place the cooked beef mixture in the pepper halves and top with cheese.

Place in the grill and cook for 30 minutes.

Serve immediately and enjoy it.

Nutrition:

Calories 422,

Total fat 22g,

Saturated fat 11g,

Total carbs 24g,

Net carbs 19g,

Protein 34g,

Sugars 11g,

Fiber 5g,

Sodium 855mg

Traeger Prime Rib Roast

Preparation Time: 10 minutes

Cooking Time: 2 hours

Servings: 8

Ingredients:

5 lb. rib roast, boneless

4 tbsp salt

1 tbsp black pepper

1-1/2 tbsp onion powder

1 tbsp granulated garlic

1 tbsp rosemary

1 cup chopped onion

1/2 cup carrots, chopped

1/2 cup celery, chopped

2 cups beef broth

Directions:

Remove the beef from the fridge 1 hour before cooking.

Preheat the Traeger to 250°F.

In a small mixing bowl, mix salt, pepper, onion, garlic, and rosemary to create your rub.

Generously coat the roast with the rub and set it aside.

Combine chopped onions, carrots, and celery in a cake pan then place the bee on top.

Place the cake pan in the middle of the Traeger and cook for 1 hour.

Pour the beef broth at the bottom of the cake pan and cook until the internal temperature reaches 120°F.

Remove the cake pan from the Traeger and let rest for 20 minutes before slicing the meat.

Pour the cooking juice through a strainer, then skim off any fat at the top.

Serve the roast with the cooking juices.

Nutrition:

Calories 721,

Total fat 60g,

Saturated fat 18g,

Total carbs 3g,

Net carbs 2g

Protein 43g,

Sugars 1g,

Fiber 1g,

Sodium 2450mmg

Fine Indian Smoked T-Bone

Preparation Time: 20 minutes

Cooking Time: 45 minutes

Servings: 12

Ingredients:

1-pound beef tenderloin, cut into 1-inch cubes

2 pounds strip steak, cut into 1-inch cubes

1 large onion, cut into 1-inch cubes

1 bell pepper, cut into 1-inch cubes

1 zucchini, cut into 1-inch cubes

10 ounces cherry tomatoes

¼ cup olive oil

½ cup steak seasoning

Directions:

Take a large bowl and add tenderloin, strip steak, onion, zucchini, bell pepper, tomatoes and mix well with olive oil

Season with steak seasoning and stir until the meat has been coated well

Cover the meat and allow it to refrigerate for 4-8 hours

Preheat your smoker to 225 degrees Fahrenheit using your desired wood

Make the kebabs by skewering meat and veggies alternatively Make sure, to begin with, meat and end with meat Transfer the skewers to your smoker rack and smoke for 45 minutes

Remove once the internal temperature reaches 135 degrees Fahrenheit (for a RARE finish)

Serve and enjoy!

Nutrition

Calories: 559

Fats: 5g

Carbs: 57g

Fiber: 1g

The South Barbacoa

Preparation Time: 15 minutes

Cooking Time: 3 hours

Servings: 10

Ingredients:

1 and ½ teaspoon pepper

1 tablespoon dried oregano

1 and ½ teaspoon cayenne pepper

1 and ½ teaspoon chili powder

1 and ½ teaspoon garlic powder

1 teaspoon ground cumin

1 teaspoon salt

3 pounds boneless beef chuck roast

Directions:

Add dampened hickory wood to your smoker and preheat to 200 degrees Fahrenheit

Take a small bowl and add oregano, cayenne pepper, black pepper, garlic powder, chili powder, cumin, salt, and seasoned salt

Mix well

Dip the chuck roast into your mixing bowl and rub the spice mix all over

Transfer the meat to your smoker and smoker for 1 and a ½ hours

Make sure to turn the meat after every 30 minutes, if you see less smoke formation, add more Pellets after every 30 minutes as well

Once the meat shows a dark red color with darkened edges, transfer the meat to a roasting pan and seal it tightly with an aluminum foil

Preheat your oven to 325 degrees Fahrenheit

Transfer the meat to your oven and bake for 1 and a ½ hours more

Shred the meat using two forks and serve!

Nutrition

Calories: 559

Fats: 5g

Carbs: 57g

Fiber: 1g

Smoked Prime Rib

Preparation Time: 25 minutes

Cooking Time: 4 hours

Servings: 12

Ingredients:

1 whole (8 pounds) prime rib roast

2 onions, thickly sliced

Smoked teriyaki marinade

Salt as needed

Fresh ground pepper as needed

Directions:

Take a large container and add meat and marinade

Combine onion slices and pour cover well

Marinade for 2 hours

Turn the meat over then cover it, refrigerate for 2 hours more Preheat your smoker to 225 degrees Fahrenheit using oak wood Remove the roast and onions from the container and discard the marinade

Skewer the onion slices making "onion lollipops" Season the rib with pepper and salt, and transfer the meat and skewered onion to your smoker rack Smoke for 4-6 hours

Remove the meat when the internal temperature reaches 135 degrees Fahrenheit

Allow it to rest for 15 minutes and serve!

Nutrition

Calories: 503 Fats: 36g

Carbs: 0g Fiber: 0.5g

Korean Beef Rib Eye

Preparation Time: 10 minutes

Cooking Time: 15 minutes

Servings: 6

Ingredients:

½ cup of soy sauce

¼ cup scallions, chopped

2 tablespoons garlic, minced

2 tablespoons Korean chili paste

1 tablespoon honey

2 teaspoons ground ginger

2 teaspoons onion powder

2 boneless rib-eye steaks, 8-12 ounces

Smoked coleslaw

12 flour tortillas

Directions:

Preheat your smoker to 200 degrees Fahrenheit with peach or pearwood

Take a small bowl and whisk in soy sauce, garlic, scallion, honey, ginger, onion powder, and mix to make the paste

Spread the paste on both sides of the steak

Transfer the steak to your smoker and smoke for 15 minutes per pound

Remove the steak when the internal temperature reaches 115 degrees Fahrenheit

Cut the steak into strips and serve with coleslaw wrapped in tortillas

Enjoy!

Nutrition

Calories: 240

Fats: 11g

Carbs: 8g

Fiber: 1g

CHAPTER 13:

Poultry Recipes

Lemon Chicken

Preparation Time: 4 hours and 30 minutes

Cooking Time: 10 minutes

Servings: 6

Ingredients:

2 teaspoons honey

1 tablespoon lemon juice

1 teaspoon lemon zest

1 clove garlic, coarsely chopped

2 sprigs thyme

Salt and pepper to taste

½ cup olive oil

6 chicken breast fillets

Directions:

Mix the honey, lemon juice, lemon zest, garlic, thyme, salt, and pepper in a bowl.

Gradually add olive oil to the mixture.

Soak the chicken fillets in the mixture.

Cover and refrigerate for 4 hours.

Preheat the Traeger wood pellet grill to 400 degrees F for 15 minutes while the lid is closed.

Grill the chicken for 5 minutes per side.

Nutrition

Calories: 140

Fats: 5g

Carbs: 6g

Fiber: 2g

Honey Garlic Chicken Wings

Preparation Time: 30 minutes

Cooking Time: 1 hour and 15 minutes

Servings: 4

Ingredients:

2 1/2 lb. chicken wings

Poultry dry rub

4 tablespoons butter

3 cloves garlic, minced

1/2 cup hot sauce

1/4 cup honey

Directions:

Sprinkle chicken wings with dry rub.

Place on a baking pan.

Set the Traeger wood pellet grill to 350 degrees F. Preheat for 15 minutes while the lid is closed. Place the baking pan on the grill. Cook for 50 minutes. Add butter to a pan over medium heat. Sauté garlic for 3 minutes. Stir in hot sauce and honey.

Cook for 5 minutes while stirring.

Coat the chicken wings with the mixture.

Grill for 10 more minutes.

Nutrition
Calories: 230
Fats: 7g
Carbs: 1g
Fiber: 2g

Cajun Chicken

Preparation Time: 15 minutes

Cooking Time: 30 minutes

Servings: 4

Ingredients:

2 lb. chicken wings

Poultry dry rub

Cajun seasoning

Directions:

Season the chicken wings with the dry rub and Cajun seasoning.

Preheat the Traeger to 350 degrees F for 15 minutes while the lid is closed.

Grill for 30 minutes, flipping twice.

Nutrition
Calories: 290
Fats: 15g
Carbs: 20g
Fiber: 1g

Chili Barbecue Chicken

Preparation Time: 5 hours and 30 minutes

Cooking Time: 2 hours and 10 minutes

 Servings: 4

Ingredients:

1 tablespoon brown sugar

1 tablespoon lime zest

1 tablespoon chili powder

1/2 teaspoon ground cumin

1/2 tablespoon ground espresso

Salt to taste

2 tablespoons olive oil

8 chicken legs

1/2 cup barbecue sauce

Directions:

Combine sugar, lime zest, chili powder, cumin, ground espresso, and salt.

Drizzle the chicken legs with oil.

Sprinkle sugar mixture all over the chicken.

Cover with foil and refrigerate for 5 hours.

Set the Traeger wood pellet grill to 180 degrees F.

Preheat it for 15 minutes while the lid is closed.

Smoke the chicken legs for 1 hour.

Increase temperature to 350 degrees F.

Grill the chicken legs for another 1 hour, flipping once.

Brush the chicken with barbecue sauce and grill for another 10 minutes.

Nutrition
Calories: 140
Fats: 5g
Carbs: 6g
Fiber: 2g

Serrano Chicken Wings

Preparation Time: 12 hours and 30 minutes

Cooking Time: 40 minutes

Servings: 4

Ingredients:

4 lb. chicken wings

2 cups beer

2 teaspoons crushed red pepper

Cajun seasoning powder

1 lb. Serrano chili peppers

1 teaspoon fresh basil

1 teaspoon dried oregano

4 cloves garlic

1 cup vinegar

Salt and pepper to taste

Directions:

Soak the chicken wings in beer.

Sprinkle it with crushed red pepper.

Cover and refrigerate for 12 hours.

Remove chicken from the brine.

Season with Cajun seasoning.

Preheat your Traeger wood pellet grill to 325 degrees F for 15 minutes while the lid is closed. Add the chicken wings and Serrano chili peppers on the grill. Grill for 5 minutes per side.

Remove chili peppers and place them in a food processor.Grill the chicken for another 20 minutes.

Add the rest of the ingredients to the food processor. Pulse until smooth.

Dip the chicken wings in the sauce.

Grill for 5 minutes and serve.

Nutrition
Calories: 140
Fats: 5g
Carbs: 6g
Fiber: 2g

Smoked Fried Chicken

Preparation Time: 1 hour and 30 minutes

Cooking Time: 3 hours

Servings: 6

Ingredients:

3.5 lb. chicken

Vegetable oil

Salt and pepper to taste

2 tablespoons hot sauce

1-quart buttermilk

2 tablespoons brown sugar

1 tablespoon poultry dry rub

2 tablespoons onion powder

2 tablespoons garlic powder

2 1/2 cups all-purpose flour

Peanut oil

Directions:

Set the Traeger wood pellet grill to 200 degrees F.

Preheat it for 15 minutes while the lid is closed.

Drizzle chicken with vegetable oil and sprinkle with salt and pepper.

Smoke chicken for 2 hours and 30 minutes.

In a bowl, mix the hot sauce, buttermilk, and sugar.

Soak the smoked chicken in the mixture.

Cover and refrigerate for 1 hour.

In another bowl, mix the dry rub, onion powder, garlic powder, and flour.

Coat the chicken with the mixture.

Heat the peanut oil in a pan over medium heat.

Fry the chicken until golden and crispy.

Nutrition
Calories: 230
Fats: 7g
Carbs: 1g
Fiber: 2g

Maple Turkey Breast

Preparation Time: 4 hours and 30 minutes

Cooking Time: 2 hours

Servings: 4

Ingredients:

3 tablespoons olive oil

3 tablespoons dark brown sugar

3 tablespoons garlic, minced

2 tablespoons Cajun seasoning

2 tablespoons Worcestershire sauce

6 lb. breast fillets

Directions:

Combine olive oil, sugar, garlic, Cajun seasoning, and Worcestershire sauce in a bowl.

Soak the turkey breast fillets in the marinade.

Cover and marinate for 4 hours.

Grill the turkey at 180 degrees F for 2 hours.

Nutrition

Calories: 290
Fats: 15g
Carbs: 20g
Fiber: 1g

Chicken Tikka Masala

Preparation Time: 12 hours and 40 minutes

Cooking Time: 1 hour

Servings: 4

Ingredients:

2 tablespoon garam masala

2 tablespoons smoked paprika

2 tablespoon ground coriander

2 tablespoon ground cumin

1 teaspoon ground cayenne pepper

1 teaspoon turmeric

1 onion, sliced

6 cloves garlic, minced

1/4 cup olive oil

1 tablespoon ginger, chopped

1 tablespoon lemon juice

1 1/2 cups Greek yogurt

1 tablespoon lime juice

1 tablespoon curry powder

Salt to taste

1 tablespoon lime juice

12 chicken drumsticks

Chopped cilantro

Directions:

Make the marinade by mixing all the spices, onion, garlic, olive oil, ginger, lemon juice, yogurt, lime juice, curry powder, and salt.Transfer to a food processor. Pulse until smooth. Divide the mixture into two. Marinade the chicken in the first bowl. Cover the bowl and refrigerate for 12 hours. Set the Traeger wood pellet grill to high. Preheat it for 15 minutes while the lid is closed. Grill the chicken for 50 minutes. Garnish with the chopped cilantro.

Nutrition
Calories: 140 Fats: 5g
Carbs: 6g Fiber: 2g

Turkey with Apricot Barbecue Glaze

Preparation Time: 30 minutes

Cooking Time: 30 minutes

Servings: 4

Ingredients:

4 turkey breast fillets

4 tablespoons chicken rub

1 cup apricot barbecue sauce

Directions:

Preheat the Traeger wood pellet grill to 365 degrees F for 15 minutes while the lid is closed.

Season the turkey fillets with the chicken run.

Grill the turkey fillets for 5 minutes per side.

Brush both sides with the barbecue sauce and grill for another 5 minutes per side.

Nutrition
Calories: 140
Fats: 5g
Carbs: 6g
Fiber: 2g

Turkey Meatballs

Preparation Time: 40 minutes

Cooking Time: 40 minutes

Servings: 8

Ingredients:

1 whole KIKOK approx. 1.5 kg

400-500 g potatoes

2-3 medium-sized onions

3-4 cloves of garlic

Rub Garlic / Chili Pepper from Traeger

Directions

Peel and boil potatoes, in the recipe there are triplets where the skin can be eaten. Cut the onions into rings and halve them, either leave the garlic cloves whole or divide them into 4-5 parts. Spread the potatoes on a baking sheet and press gently until flat, spread the garlic and onions over the potatoes. Remove the back from the KIKOK and season the chicken from both sides. Place the KIKOK on the potatoes and Traeger smoke for about 30 minutes at about 100 ° C, then the temperature to 190 ° C and heat a barbecue to a core temperature of 80 ° C. The potatoes catch the leaked fat and become wonderfully "choppy", making them crispy from below. If you have now used potatoes without their skins, you can process them into the puree and serve them gratinated with cheese to serve with the chicken

Nutrition

Calories: 230
Fats: 7g
Carbs: 1g
Fiber: 2g

Herb Roasted Turkey

Preparation time: 15 minutes

Cooking time: 3 hours and 30 minutes

Servings: 12

Ingredients:

14 pounds turkey, cleaned

2 tablespoons chopped mixed herbs

Pork and poultry rub as needed

1/4 teaspoon ground black pepper

3 tablespoons butter, unsalted, melted

8 tablespoons butter, unsalted, softened

2 cups chicken broth

Directions:

Clean the turkey by removing the giblets, wash it inside out, pat dry with paper towels, then place it on a roasting pan and tuck the turkey wings by tiring with butcher's string.

Switch on the Traeger grill, fill the grill hopper with hickory flavored wood pellets, power the grill on by using the control panel, select 'smoke' on the temperature dial, or set the temperature to 325 degrees F and let it preheat for a minimum of 15 minutes.

Meanwhile, prepare herb butter and for this, take a small bowl, place the softened butter in it, add black pepper and mixed herbs and beat until fluffy.

Place some of the prepared herb butter underneath the skin of the turkey by using a handle of a wooden spoon, and massage the skin to distribute butter evenly.

Then rub the exterior of the turkey with melted butter, season with pork and poultry rub, and pour the broth in the roasting pan.

When the grill has preheated, open the lid, place a roasting pan containing turkey on the grill grate, shut the grill, and smoke for 3 hours and 30 minutes until the internal temperature reaches 165 degrees F and the top has turned golden brown.

When done, transfer turkey to a cutting board, let it rest for 30 minutes, then carve it into slices and serve.

Nutrition

Calories: 154.6 Cal

Fat: 3.1 g

Carbs: 8.4 g

Protein: 28.8 g

Fiber: 0.4 g

Turkey Legs

Preparation time: 24 hours

Cooking time: 5 hours

Servings: 4

Ingredients:

4 turkey legs

For the Brine:

1/2 cup curing salt

1 tablespoon whole black peppercorns

1 cup BBQ rub

1/2 cup brown sugar

2 bay leaves

2 teaspoons liquid smoke

16 cups of warm water

4 cups ice

8 cups of cold water

Directions:

Prepare the brine and for this, take a large stockpot, place it over high heat, pour warm water in it, add peppercorn, bay leaves, and liquid smoke, stir in salt, sugar, and BBQ rub and bring it to a boil. Remove pot from heat, bring it to room temperature, then pour in cold water, add ice cubes and let the brine chill in the refrigerator. Then add turkey legs in it, submerge them completely, and let soak for 24 hours in the refrigerator. After 24 hours, remove turkey legs from the brine, rinse well and pat dry with paper towels. When ready to cook, switch on the Traeger grill, fill the grill hopper with hickory flavored wood pellets, power the grill on by using the control panel, select 'smoke' on the temperature dial, or set the temperature to 250 degrees F and let it preheat for a minimum of 15 minutes. When the grill has preheated, open the lid, place turkey legs on the grill grate, shut the grill, and smoke for 5 hours until nicely browned and the internal temperature reaches 165 degrees F. Serve immediately.

Nutrition

Calories: 416 Cal

Fat: 13.3 g

Carbs: 0 g

Protein: 69.8 g

Fiber: 0 g

Turkey Breast

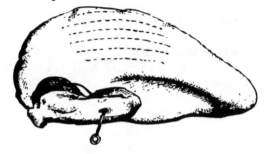

Preparation time: 12 hours

Cooking time: 8 hours

Servings: 6

Ingredients:

For the Brine:

2 pounds turkey breast, deboned

2 tablespoons ground black pepper

1/4 cup salt

1 cup brown sugar

4 cups cold water

For the BBQ Rub:

2 tablespoons dried onions

2 tablespoons garlic powder

1/4 cup paprika

2 tablespoons ground black pepper

1 tablespoon salt

2 tablespoons brown sugar

2 tablespoons red chili powder

2 tablespoons sugar

2 tablespoons ground cumin

Directions:

Prepare the brine and for this, take a large bowl, add salt, black pepper, and sugar in it, pour in water, and stir until sugar has dissolved.

Place turkey breast in it, submerge it completely, and let it soak for a minimum of 12 hours in the refrigerator.

Meanwhile, prepare the BBQ rub and for this, take a small bowl, place all of its ingredients in it and then stir until combined, set aside until required.

Then remove turkey breast from the brine and season well with the prepared BBQ rub.

When ready to cook, switch on the Traeger grill, fill the grill hopper with apple-flavored wood pellets, power the grill on by using the control panel, select 'smoke' on the temperature dial, or set the temperature to 180 degrees F and let it preheat for a minimum of 15 minutes.

When the grill has preheated, open the lid, place turkey breast on the grill grate, shut the grill, change the smoking temperature to 225 degrees F, and smoke for 8 hours until the internal temperature reaches 160 degrees F.

When done, transfer turkey to a cutting board, let it rest for 10 minutes, then cut it into slices and serve.

Nutrition

Calories: 250 Cal

Fat: 5 g

Carbs: 31 g

Protein: 18 g

Fiber: 5 g

Spicy BBQ Chicken

Preparation time: 8 hours and 10 minutes

Cooking time: 3 hours

Servings: 6

Ingredients:

1 whole chicken, cleaned

For the Marinade:

1 medium white onion, peeled

6 Thai chilies

5 cloves of garlic, peeled

1 scotch bonnet

3 tablespoons salt

2 tablespoons sugar

2 tablespoons sweet paprika

4 cups grapeseed oil

Directions:

Prepare the marinade, and for this, place all of its ingredients in a food processor and pulse for 2 minutes until smooth.

Smoother whole chicken with the prepared marinade and let it marinate in the refrigerator for a minimum of 8 hours.

When ready to cook, switch on the Traeger grill, fill the grill hopper with apple-flavored wood pellets, power the grill on by using the control panel, select 'smoke' on the temperature dial, or set the temperature to 300 degrees F and let it preheat for a minimum of 15 minutes. When the grill has preheated, open the lid, place chicken on the grill grate breast-side up, shut the grill, and smoke for 3 hours until the internal temperature of chicken reaches 165 degrees F. When done, transfer chicken to a cutting board, let it rest for 15 minutes, then cut into slices and serve.

Nutrition

Calories: 100 Cal

Fat: 2.8 g

Carbs: 13 g

Protein: 3.5 g

Fiber: 2 g

Teriyaki Wings

Preparation time: 8 hours

Cooking time: 50 minutes

Servings: 8

Ingredients:

2 ½ pounds large chicken wings

1 tablespoon toasted sesame seeds

For the Marinade:

2 scallions, sliced

2 tablespoons grated ginger

½ teaspoon minced garlic

1/4 cup brown sugar

1/2 cup soy sauce

2 tablespoon rice wine vinegar

2 teaspoons sesame oil

1/4 cup water

Directions:

Prepare the chicken wings and for this, remove tips from the wings, cut each chicken wing through the joint into three pieces, and then place in a large plastic bag.

Prepare the sauce and for this, take a small saucepan, place it over medium-high heat, add all of its ingredients in it, stir until mixed, and bring it to a boil.

Then switch heat to medium level, simmer the sauce for 10 minutes, and when done, cool the sauce completely.

Pour the sauce over chicken wings, seal the bag, turn it upside down to coat chicken wings with the sauce and let it marinate for a minimum of 8 hours in the refrigerator.

When ready to cook, switch on the Traeger grill, fill the grill hopper with maple-flavored wood pellets, power the grill on by using the control panel, select 'smoke' on the temperature dial, or set the temperature to 350 degrees F and let it preheat for a minimum of 15 minutes.

Meanwhile,

When the grill has preheated, open the lid, place chicken wings on the grill grate, shut the grill, and smoke for 50 minutes until crispy and meat is no longer pink, turning halfway.

When done, transfer chicken wings to a dish, sprinkle with sesame seeds, then serve.

Nutrition

Calories: 150 Cal

Fat: 7.5 g

Carbs: 6 g

Protein: 12 g

CHAPTER 14:

Fish Recipes

Jerk Shrimp

Preparation time: 15 minutes

Cooking time: 6

Servings: 12

Ingredients:

2 pounds shrimp, peeled, deveined

3 tablespoons olive oil

For the Spice Mix:

1 teaspoon garlic powder

1 teaspoon of sea salt

1/4 teaspoon ground cayenne

1 tablespoon brown sugar

1/8 teaspoon smoked paprika

1 tablespoon smoked paprika

1/4 teaspoon ground thyme

1 lime, zested

Directions:

Switch on the Traeger grill, fill the grill hopper with flavored wood pellets, power the grill on by using the control panel, select 'smoke' on the temperature dial, or set the temperature to 450 degrees F and let it preheat for a minimum of 5 minutes.

Meanwhile, prepare the spice mix and for this, take a small bowl, place all of its ingredients in it and stir until mixed.

Take a large bowl, place shrimps in it, sprinkle with prepared spice mix, drizzle with oil and toss until well coated.

When the grill has preheated, open the lid, place shrimps on the grill grate, shut the grill, and smoke for 3 minutes per side until firm and thoroughly cooked.

When done, transfer shrimps to a dish and then serve.

Nutrition

Calories: 131 Cal

Fat: 4.3 g

Carbs: 0 g

Protein: 22 g

Fiber: 0 g

Spicy Shrimps Skewers

Preparation time: 10 minutes

Cooking time: 6 minutes

Servings: 4

Ingredients:

2 pounds shrimp, peeled, and deveined

For the Marinade:

6 ounces Thai chilies

6 cloves of garlic, peeled

1 ½ teaspoon sugar

2 tablespoons Napa Valley rub

1 ½ tablespoon white vinegar

3 tablespoons olive oil

Directions:

Prepare the marinade and for this, place all of its ingredients in a food processor and then pulse for 1 minute until smooth.

Take a large bowl, place shrimps on it, add prepared marinade, toss until well coated, and let marinate for a minimum of 30 minutes in the refrigerator.

When ready to cook, switch on the Traeger grill, fill the grill hopper with apple-flavored wood pellets, power the grill on by using the control panel, select 'smoke' on the temperature dial, or set the temperature to 450 degrees F and let it preheat for a minimum of 5 minutes.

Meanwhile, remove shrimps from the marinade and then thread onto skewers.

When the grill has preheated, open the lid, place shrimps' skewers on the grill grate, shut the grill, and smoke for 3 minutes per side until firm.

When done, transfer shrimps' skewers to a dish and then serve.

Nutrition

Calories: 187.2 Cal

Fat: 2.7 g

Carbs: 2.7 g

Protein: 23.2 g

Fiber: 0.2 g

Tuna Tacos

Preparation time: 10 minutes

Cooking time: 35 minutes

Servings: 4

Ingredients:

1.5 kg of tuna

3 tablespoons of olive oil

1/4 cup of spices for fish

1 piece of grated ginger root

3 tablespoons of vinegar

1 tablespoon of honey

1 teaspoon of red pepper flakes

1/2 teaspoon of salt

1/4 teaspoon ground black pepper

1 fresh anna (already cleaned and finely chopped)

1 cabbage (grated)

2 carrots (grated)

12 tortillas (you can also use the piadina)

3 spoons of cilantro (chopped)

Preparation

Preheat the barbecue to 230 ° C and prepare it for the grill, close the lid, and leave it for about 15 minutes. Brush the tuna with a light layer of olive oil and then cover it with a layer of spice for fish, let the tuna marinate for 10 minutes while preparing the cabbage salad. For the salad, mix ginger, vinegar, honey, the pepper flakes, salt, and pepper, then in a large bowl combined with the pineapple, carrots, and cabbage. Grate the tuna for 3 minutes on each side, then remove it from the grill and let it rest for 5 minutes before continuing to fray it. At this point you can fill the tortillas (or piadina) with tuna and coleslaw, the tacos are ready to serve them!!

Nutrition

Calories: 290 Cal Fat: 22 g

Carbs: 1 g Protein: 20 g Fiber: 0.3 g

Lemon Garlic Scallops

Preparation time: 10 minutes

Cooking time: 5 minutes

Servings: 6

Ingredients:

1 dozen scallops

2 tablespoons chopped parsley

Salt as needed

1 tablespoon olive oil

1 tablespoon butter, unsalted

1 teaspoon lemon zest

For the Garlic Butter:

½ teaspoon minced garlic

1 lemon, juiced

4 tablespoons butter, unsalted, melted

Directions:

Switch on the Traeger grill, fill the grill hopper with alder flavored wood pellets, power the grill on by using the control panel, select 'smoke' on the temperature dial, or set the temperature to 400 degrees F and let it preheat for a minimum of 15 minutes. Meanwhile, remove the grill from scallops, pat dry with paper towels, and then season with salt and black pepper. When the grill has preheated, open the lid, place a skillet on the grill grate, add butter and oil, and when the butter melts, place seasoned scallops on it and then cook for 2 minutes until seared. Meanwhile, prepare the garlic butter and for this, take a small bowl, place all of its ingredients in it and then whisk until combined. Flip the scallops, top with some of the prepared garlic butter, and cook for another minute. When done, transfer scallops to a dish, top with remaining garlic butter, sprinkle with parsley and lemon zest and then serve.

Nutrition

Calories: 184 Cal Fat: 10 g

Carbs: 1 g Protein: 22 g

Fiber: 0.2 g

Halibut in Parchment

Preparation time: 15 minutes

Cooking time: 15 minutes

Servings: 4

Ingredients:

16 asparagus spears, trimmed, sliced into 1/2-inch pieces

2 ears of corn kernels

4 ounces halibut fillets, pin bones removed

2 lemons, cut into 12 slices

Salt as needed

Ground black pepper as needed

2 tablespoons olive oil

2 tablespoons chopped parsley

Directions:

Switch on the Traeger grill, fill the grill hopper with flavored wood pellets, power the grill on by using the control panel, select 'smoke' on the temperature dial, or set the temperature to 450 degrees F and let it preheat for a minimum of 5 minutes. Meanwhile, cut out 18-inch long parchment paper, place a fillet in the center of each parchment, season with salt and black pepper, and then drizzle with oil. Cover each fillet with three lemon slices, overlapping slightly, sprinkle one-fourth of asparagus and corn on each fillet, season with some salt and black pepper, and seal the fillets and vegetables tightly to prevent steam from escaping the packet. When the grill has preheated, open the lid, place fillet packets on the grill grate, shut the grill, and smoke for 15 minutes until packets have turned slightly brown and puffed up. When done, transfer packets to a dish, let them stand for 5 minutes, then cut 'X' in the center of each packet, carefully uncover the fillets and vegetables, sprinkle with parsley, and then serve.

Nutrition

Calories: 186.6 Cal

Fat: 2.8 g

Carbs: 14.2 g

Protein: 25.7 g

Fiber: 4.1 g

Chilean Sea Bass

Preparation time: 30 minutes

Cooking time: 40 minutes

Servings: 6

Ingredients:

4 sea bass fillets, skinless, each about 6 ounces

Chicken rub as needed

8 tablespoons butter, unsalted

2 tablespoons chopped thyme leaves

Lemon slices for serving

For the Marinade:

1 lemon, juiced

4 teaspoons minced garlic

1 tablespoon chopped thyme

1 teaspoon blackened rub

1 tablespoon chopped oregano

1/4 cup oil

Directions:

Prepare the marinade and for this, take a small bowl, place all of its ingredients in it, stir until well combined, and then pour the mixture into a large plastic bag. Add fillets in the bag, seal it, turn it upside down to coat fillets with the marinade and let it marinate for a minimum of 30 minutes in the refrigerator. When ready to cook, switch on the Traeger grill, fill the grill hopper with apple-flavored wood pellets, power the grill on by using the control panel, select 'smoke' on the temperature dial, or set the temperature to 325 degrees F and let it preheat for a minimum of 15 minutes. Meanwhile, take a large baking pan and place butter on it. When the grill has preheated, open the lid, place the baking pan on the grill grate, and wait until butter melts. When done, transfer fillets to a dish, sprinkle with thyme, then serve with lemon slices.

Nutrition

Calories: 232 Cal

Fat: 12.2 g

Carbs: 0.8 g

Protein: 28.2 g

Fiber: 0.1 g

Sriracha Salmon

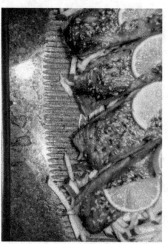

Preparation time: 2 hours and 10 minutes

Cooking time: 25 minutes

Servings: 4

Ingredients:

3-pound salmon, skin on

For the Marinade:

1 teaspoon lime zest

1 tablespoon minced garlic

1 tablespoon grated ginger

Sea salt as needed

Ground black pepper as needed

1/4 cup maple syrup

2 tablespoons soy sauce

2 tablespoons Sriracha sauce

1 tablespoon toasted sesame oil

1 tablespoon rice vinegar

1 teaspoon toasted sesame seeds

Directions:

Prepare the marinade and for this, take a small bowl, place all of its ingredients in it, stir until well combined, and then pour the mixture into a large plastic bag.

Add salmon in the bag, seal it, turn it upside down to coat salmon with the marinade and let it marinate for a minimum of 2 hours in the refrigerator.

When ready to cook, switch on the Traeger grill, fill the grill hopper with flavored wood pellets, power the grill on by using the control panel, select 'smoke' on the temperature dial, or set the temperature to 450 degrees F and let it preheat for a minimum of 5 minutes.

Meanwhile, take a large baking sheet, line it with parchment paper, place salmon on it skin-side down and then brush with the marinade.

When the grill has preheated, open the lid, place a baking sheet containing salmon on the grill grate, shut the grill, and smoke for 25 minutes until thoroughly cooked.

When done, transfer salmon to a dish and then serve.

Nutrition

Calories: 360 Cal

Fat: 21 g

Carbs: 28 g

Protein: 16 g

Fiber: 1.5 g

Grilled Rainbow Trout

Preparation time: 1 hour

Cooking time: 2 hours

Servings: 6

Ingredients:

6 rainbow trout, cleaned, butterfly

For the Brine:

1/4 cup salt

1 tablespoon ground black pepper

1/2 cup brown sugar

2 tablespoons soy sauce

16 cups water

Directions:

Prepare the brine and for this, take a large container, add all of its ingredients in it, stir until sugar has dissolved, then add trout and let soak for 1 hour in the refrigerator.

When ready to cook, switch on the Traeger grill, fill the grill hopper with oak flavored wood pellets, power the grill on by using the control panel, select 'smoke' on the temperature dial, or set the temperature to 225 degrees F and let it preheat for a minimum of 15 minutes.

Meanwhile, remove trout from the brine and pat dry with paper towels.

When the grill has preheated, open the lid, place trout on the grill grate, shut the grill, and smoke for 2 hours until thoroughly cooked and tender.

When done, transfer trout to a dish and then serve.

Nutrition

Calories: 250 Cal

Fat: 12 g

Carbs: 1.4 g

Protein: 33 g

Fiber: 0.3 g

Cider Salmon

Preparation time: 9 hours

Cooking time: 1 hour

Servings: 4

Ingredients:

1 ½ pound salmon fillet, skin-on, center-cut, pin bone removed

For the Brine:

4 juniper berries, crushed

1 bay leaf, crumbled

1-piece star anise, broken

1 1/2 cups apple cider

For the Cure:

1/2 cup salt

1 teaspoon ground black pepper

1/4 cup brown sugar

2 teaspoons barbecue rub

Directions:

Prepare the brine and for this, take a large container, add all of its ingredients in it, stir until mixed, then add salmon and let soak for a minimum of 8 hours in the refrigerator.

Meanwhile, prepare the cure and for this, take a small bowl, place all of its ingredients in it and stir until combined.

After 8 hours, remove salmon from the brine, then take a baking dish, place half of the cure in it, top with salmon skin-side down, sprinkle remaining cure on top, cover with plastic wrap and let it rest for 1 hour in the refrigerator.

When ready to cook, switch on the Traeger grill, fill the grill hopper with oak flavored wood pellets, power the grill on by using the control panel, select 'smoke' on the temperature dial, or set the temperature to 200 degrees F and let it preheat for a minimum of 5 minutes.

Meanwhile, remove salmon from the cure, pat dry with paper towels, and then sprinkle with black pepper.

When the grill has preheated, open the lid, place salmon on the grill grate, shut the grill, and smoke for 1 hour until the internal temperature reaches 150 degrees F.

When done, transfer salmon to a cutting board, let it rest for 5 minutes, then remove the skin and serve.

Nutrition

Calories: 233 Cal

Fat: 14 g

Carbs: 0 g

Protein: 25 g

Octopus with Lemon and Oregano

Preparation Time: 15 minutes

Cooking Time: 1 hour and 30 minutes

Servings: 4

Ingredients:

3 lemons

3 pounds cleaned octopus, thawed if frozen

6 cloves garlic, peeled

4 sprigs of fresh oregano

2 bay leaves

Salt and pepper

3 tablespoons good-quality olive oil

Minced fresh oregano for garnish

Directions:

Halve one of the lemons. Put the octopus, garlic, oregano sprigs, bay leaves, a large pinch of salt, and lemon halves in a large pot with enough water to cover by a couple of inches. Bring to a boil, adjust the heat so the liquid bubbles gently but steadily, and cook, occasionally turning with tongs, until the octopus is tender 30 to 90 minutes. (Check with the tip of a sharp knife; it should go in smoothly.) Drain; discard the seasonings. (You can cover and refrigerate the octopus for up to 24 hours.)

Start the coals or heat a gas grill for direct hot cooking. Make sure the grates are clean.

Squeeze the juice 1 of the remaining lemons and whisk it with the oil and salt and pepper to taste. Cut the octopus into large serving pieces and toss with the oil mixture.

Put the octopus on the grill directly over the fire. Cover the grill and cook until heated through and charred, 4 to 5 minutes per side. Cut the remaining lemon into wedges. Transfer the octopus to a platter, sprinkle with minced oregano, and serve with the lemon wedges.

Nutrition:

Calories: 139

Fats: 1.8 g

Cholesterol: 0 mg

Carbohydrates: 3.7 g

Fiber: 0 g

Sugars: 0 g

Proteins: 25.4 g

Mussels with Pancetta Aïoli

Preparation Time: 15 minutes

Cooking Time: 30 minutes

Servings: 4

Ingredients:

¾ cup mayonnaise (to make your own, see page 460)

1 tablespoon minced garlic, or more to taste

1 4-ounce slice pancetta, chopped

Salt and pepper

4 pounds mussels

8 thick slices of Italian bread

¼ cup good-quality olive oil

Directions:

Whisk the mayonnaise and garlic together in a small bowl. Put the pancetta in a small cold skillet, turn the heat to low; cook, occasionally stir, until most of the fat is rendered and the meat turns golden and crisp about 5 minutes. Drain on a paper towel, then stir into the mayonnaise along with 1 teaspoon of the rendered fat from the pan. Taste and add more garlic and some salt if you like. Cover and refrigerate until you're ready to serve. (You can make the aïoli up to several days ahead; refrigerate in an airtight container.)

Start the coals or heat a gas grill for direct hot cooking. Make sure the grates are clean.

Rinse the mussels and pull off any beards. Discard any that are broken or don't close when tapped.

Brush both sides of the bread slices with the oil. Put the bread on the grill directly over the fire. Close the lid and toast, turning once, until it develops grill marks with some charring, 1 to 2 minutes per side. Remove from the grill and keep warm.

Scatter the mussels onto the grill directly over the fire, spreading them out, so they are in a single layer. Immediately close the lid and cook for 3 minutes. Transfer the open mussels to a large bowl with tongs. If any have not opened, leave them on the grill, close the lid, and cook for another minute or 2, checking frequently and removing open mussels until they are all off the grill.

Dollop the aioli over the tops of the mussels and use a large spoon to turn them over to coat them. Serve the mussels drizzled with their juices, either over (or alongside) the bread.

Nutrition:

Calories: 159

Fats: 6.1 g

Cholesterol: 0 mg

Carbohydrates: 14.95 g

Fiber: 0 g

Sugars: 0 g

Proteins: 9.57 g

Mango Shrimp

Preparation Time: 0 minutes

Cooking Time: 15 minutes

Servings: 4

Ingredients:

1 lb. shrimp, peeled and deveined but tail intact

2 tablespoons olive oil

Mango seasoning

Directions:

Turn on your wood pellet grill.

Preheat it to 425 degrees F.

Coat the shrimp with the oil and season with the mango seasoning.

Thread the shrimp into skewers.

Grill for 3 minutes per side.

Serving Suggestion: Garnish with chopped parsley.

Tip: Soak the wooden skewers in water before grilling.

Nutrition:

Calories: 223.1

Fat: 4.3 g

Cholesterol: 129.2 mg

Carbohydrates: 29.2 g

Fiber: 4.4 g

Sugars: 15. 6g

Protein: 19.5 g

Blackened Salmon

Preparation Time: 0 minutes

Cooking Time: 30 minutes

 Servings: 4

Ingredients:

2 lb. salmon, fillet, scaled and deboned

2 tablespoons olive oil

4 tablespoons sweet dry rub

1 tablespoon cayenne pepper

2 cloves garlic, minced

Directions:

Turn on your wood pellet grill.

Set it to 350 degrees F.

Brush the salmon with the olive oil.

Sprinkle it with the dry rub, cayenne pepper, and garlic.

Grill for 5 minutes per side.

Nutrition:

Calories: 460

Fat: 23 g

Cholesterol: 140 mg

Carbohydrates: 7 g

Fiber: 5 g

Sugars: 2 g

Protein: 50 g

Blackened Catfish

Preparation Time: 0 minutes

Cooking Time: 40 minutes

Servings: 4

Ingredients:

Spice blend

1 teaspoon granulated garlic

1/4 teaspoon cayenne pepper

1/2 cup Cajun seasoning

1 teaspoon ground thyme

1 teaspoon ground oregano

1 teaspoon onion powder

1 tablespoon smoked paprika

1 teaspoon pepper

Fish

4 catfish fillets

Salt to taste

1/2 cup butter

Directions:

In a bowl, combine all the ingredients for the spice blend.

Sprinkle both sides of the fish with the salt and spice blend.

Set your wood pellet grill to 450 degrees F.

Heat your cast iron pan and add the butter. Add the fillets to the pan. Cook for 5 minutes per side. Serving Suggestion: Garnish with lemon wedges. Tip: Smoke the catfish for 20 minutes before seasoning.

Nutrition

Calories: 181.5

Fat: 10.5 g

Cholesterol: 65.8 mg

Carbohydrates: 2.9 g

Fiber: 1.8 g

Sugars: 0.4 g

Protein: 19.2 g

Bacon-Wrapped Scallops

Preparation Time: 0 minutes

Cooking Time: 30 minutes

Servings: 4

Ingredients:

12 scallops

12 bacon slices

3 tablespoons lemon juice

Pepper to taste

Directions:

Turn on your wood pellet grill.

Set it to smoke.

Let it burn for 5 minutes while the lid is open.

Set it to 400 degrees F.

Wrap the scallops with bacon.

Secure with a toothpick.

Drizzle with the lemon juice and season with pepper.

Add the scallops to a baking tray.

Place the tray on the grill.

Grill for 20 minutes.

Serving Suggestion: Serve with sweet chili sauce.

Nutrition:

Calories: 180.3

Fat: 8 g

Cholesterol: 590.2 mg

Carbohydrates: 3 g

Fiber: 0 g

Sugars: 0 g

Protein: 22 g

Cajun Seasoned Shrimp

Preparation Time: 10 minutes

Cooking Time: 16-20 Minutes

Servings: 4

Ingredients:

20 pieces of jumbo Shrimp

1/2 teaspoon of Cajun seasoning

1 tablespoon of Canola oil

Directions:

Mix well for fine coating.

Now put the shrimp on skewers.

Put the grill grate inside the grill and set a timer to 8 minutes at high for preheating.

Once the grill is preheated, open the unit and place the shrimp skewers inside.

Cook the shrimp for 2 minutes.

Open the unit to flip the shrimp and cook for another 2 minutes at medium.

Own done, serve.

Nutrition:

Calories: 382

Total Fat: 7.4g

Saturated Fat: 0g

Cholesterol: 350mg

Sodium: 2208mg

Total Carbohydrate: 23.9g

Dietary Fiber 2.6g

Total Sugars: 2.6g

Protein: 50.2g

Juicy Smoked Salmon

Preparation Time: 6 hours

Cooking Time: 50 minutes

Servings: 5

Ingredients:

½ cup of sugar

2 tablespoon salt

2 tablespoons crushed red pepper flakes

½ cup fresh mint leaves, chopped

¼ cup brandy

1 (4 pounds) salmon, bones removed

2 cups alder wood pellets, soaked in water

Directions:

Take a medium-sized bowl and add brown sugar, crushed red pepper flakes, mint leaves, salt, and brandy until a paste form

Rub the paste all over your salmon and wrap the salmon with a plastic wrap

Allow them to chill overnight

Preheat your smoker to 220 degrees Fahrenheit and add wood Pellets

Transfer the salmon to the smoker rack and cook smoke for 45 minutes

Once the salmon has turned red-brown and the flesh flakes off easily, take it out and serve!

Nutrition:

Calories: 370

Fats: 28g

Carbs: 1g

Fiber: 0g

CHAPTER 15:

Vegetable Recipes

Grilled Green Beans

Preparation Time: 5 minutes

Cooking Time: 20 minutes

Servings: 3

Ingredients:

1 Pound of fresh Green Beans

4 Strips of cut into small pieces of Bacon

4 tablespoons of extra-virgin olive oil

2 Minced Garlic Cloves

1 teaspoon of kosher salt

Directions:

When you are ready to cook, set the temperature of the grill to high and preheat with the lid closed for about 15 minutes

Toss all your ingredients together and spread it out evenly over a clean sheet tray.

Place the tray over the grill grate and grill for about 20 Minutes

Serve and enjoy your dish!

Nutrition

Calories: 68,

 Fat: 4g,

Carbohydrates: 0 g,

Dietary Fiber: 0g,

Protein: 0g

Grilled Asparagus

Preparation Time: 5 minutes

Cooking Time: 20 minutes

Servings: 4

Ingredients:

3 cups of vegetables sliced

2 tbsp of olive oil

2 tbsp of garlic & herb seasoning

Directions:

Preheat your Traeger grill to a temperature of about 350°F

While your Traeger is heating, slice the vegetables. Cut the spears from the Broccoli and the Zucchini; then wash the outsides and slice into spears, Cut the peppers into wide strips. You can also grill carrots, corn, asparagus, and potatoes. Grill at a temperature of about 350°F for about 20 minutes. Serve and enjoy!

Nutrition

Calories: 47,

 Fat: 3g,

Carbohydrates: 1g,

Dietary Fiber: 1g,

Protein: 2.2g

Traeger Grill Eggplants

Preparation Time: 5 minutes

Cooking Time: 12 minutes

Servings: 6

Ingredients:

1 to 2 large eggplants

3 tablespoons of extra virgin olive oil

2 tablespoons of balsamic vinegar

2 finely minced garlic cloves

1 pinch of each thyme, dill; oregano, and basil

Directions:

Gather your ingredients.

Heat your Traeger grill to a medium-high

When the Traeger grill becomes hot; slice the eggplant into slices of about 1/2-inch of thickness

In a bowl, whisk all together with the olive oil with the balsamic vinegar, the garlic, the herbs, the salt, and the pepper.

Brush both sides of the sliced eggplant with oil and with the vinegar mixture.

Place the eggplant over the preheated grill

Grill the eggplant for about 12 minutes

Serve and enjoy!

Nutrition

Calories: 56,

Fat: 0.8g,

Carbohydrates: 11g,

Dietary Fiber: 4.1g,

Protein: 4g

Green Beans with Bacon

Preparation time: 10 minutes

Cooking time: 20 minutes

Servings: 6

Ingredients:

4 strips of bacon, chopped

1 1/2-pound green beans, ends trimmed

1 teaspoon minced garlic

1 teaspoon salt

4 tablespoons olive oil

Directions:

Switch on the Traeger grill, fill the grill hopper with flavored wood pellets, power the grill on by using the control panel, select 'smoke' on the temperature dial, or set the temperature to 450 degrees F and let it preheat for a minimum of 15 minutes. Meanwhile, take a sheet tray, place all the ingredients in it and toss until mixed. When the grill has preheated, open the lid, place the prepared sheet tray on the grill grate, shut the grill, and smoke for 20 minutes until lightly browned and cooked. When done, transfer green beans to a dish and then serve.

Nutrition

Calories: 93 Cal

Fat: 4.6 g

Carbs: 8.2 g

Protein: 5.9 g

Fiber: 2.9 g

Grilled Potato Salad

Preparation time: 15 minutes

Cooking time: 10 minutes

Servings: 8

Ingredients:

1 ½ pound fingerling potatoes, halved lengthwise

1 small jalapeno, sliced

10 scallions

2 teaspoons salt

2 tablespoons rice vinegar

2 teaspoons lemon juice

2/3 cup olive oil, divided

Directions:

Switch on the Traeger grill, fill the grill hopper with pecan flavored wood pellets, power the grill on by using the control panel, select 'smoke' on the temperature dial, or set the temperature to 450 degrees F and let it preheat for a minimum of 5 minutes. Meanwhile, prepare scallions, and for this, brush them with some oil. When the grill has preheated, open the lid, place scallions on the grill grate, shut the grill, and smoke for 3 minutes until lightly charred. Then transfer scallions to a cutting board, let them cool for 5 minutes, then cut into slices and set aside until required. Brush potatoes with some oil, season with some salt and black pepper, place potatoes on the grill grate, shut the grill, and smoke for 5 minutes until thoroughly cooked. Then take a large bowl, pour in remaining oil, add salt, lemon juice, and vinegar and stir until combined. Add grilled scallion and potatoes, toss until well mixed, taste to adjust seasoning, and then serve.

Nutrition

Calories: 223.7 Cal

Fat: 12 g

Carbs: 27 g

Protein: 1.9 g

Fiber: 3.3 g

Vegetable Sandwich

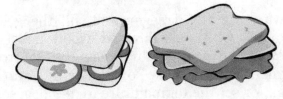

Preparation time: 30 minutes

Cooking time: 45 minutes

Servings: 4

Ingredients: For the Smoked Hummus:

1 1/2 cups cooked chickpeas

1 tablespoon minced garlic

1 teaspoon salt

4 tablespoons lemon juice

2 tablespoon olive oil

1/3 cup tahini

For the Vegetables:

2 large portobello mushrooms

1 small eggplant, destemmed, sliced into strips

1 teaspoon salt

1 small zucchini, trimmed, sliced into strips

½ teaspoon ground black pepper

1 small yellow squash, peeled, sliced into strips

¼ cup olive oil

For the Cheese:

1 lemon, juiced

½ teaspoon minced garlic

¼ teaspoon ground black pepper

¼ teaspoon salt

1/2 cup ricotta cheese

To Assemble:

1 bunch basil, leaves chopped

2 heirloom tomatoes, sliced

4 ciabatta buns, halved

Directions:

Switch on the Traeger grill, fill the grill hopper with pecan flavored wood pellets, power the grill on by using the control panel, select 'smoke' on the temperature dial, or set the temperature to 180 degrees F and let it preheat for a minimum of 15 minutes.

Meanwhile, prepare the hummus, and for this, take a sheet tray and spread chickpeas on it.

When the grill has preheated, open the lid, place sheet tray on the grill grate, shut the grill, and smoke for 20 minutes.

When done, transfer chickpeas to a food processor, add remaining ingredients for the hummus in it and pulse for 2 minutes until smooth, set aside until required.

Change the smoking temperature to 500 degrees F, shut with lid, and let it preheat for 10 minutes.

Meanwhile, prepare vegetables and for this, take a large bowl, place all the vegetables in it, add salt and black pepper, drizzle with oil and lemon juice and toss until coated.

Place vegetables on the grill grate, shut with lid, then smoke for eggplant, zucchini, and squash for 15 minutes and mushrooms for 25 minutes.

Meanwhile, prepare the cheese and for this, take a small bowl, place all of its ingredients in it and stir until well combined. Assemble the sandwich for this, cut buns in half lengthwise, spread prepared hummus on one side, spread cheese on the other side, then stuff with grilled vegetables and top with tomatoes and basil. Serve straight away.

Nutrition

Calories: 560 Cal

Fat: 40 g

Carbs: 45 g

Protein: 8.3 g

Fiber: 6.8 g

Grilled Zucchini

Preparation time: 5 minutes

Cooking time: 10 minutes

Servings: 6

Ingredients:

4 medium zucchinis

2 tablespoons olive oil

1 tablespoon sherry vinegar

2 sprigs of thyme, leaves chopped

½ teaspoon salt

1/3 teaspoon ground black pepper

Directions:

Switch on the Traeger grill, fill the grill hopper with oak flavored wood pellets, power the grill on by using the control panel, select 'smoke' on the temperature dial, or set the temperature to 350 degrees F and let it preheat for a minimum of 5 minutes. Meanwhile, cut the ends of each zucchini, cut each in half and then into thirds, and place in a plastic bag. Add remaining ingredients, seal the bag, and shake well to coat zucchini pieces. When the grill has preheated, open the lid, place zucchini on the grill grate, shut the grill, and smoke for 4 minutes per side. When done, transfer zucchini to a dish, garnish with more thyme and then serve.

Nutrition

Calories: 74 Cal Fat: 5.4 g

Carbs: 6.1 g Protein: 2.6 g Fiber: 2.3 g

Grilled Sugar Snap Peas

Preparation time: 15 minutes

Cooking time: 10 minutes

Servings: 4

Ingredients:

2-pound sugar snap peas end trimmed

½ teaspoon garlic powder

1 teaspoon salt

2/3 teaspoon ground black pepper

2 tablespoons olive oil

Directions:

Switch on the Traeger grill, fill the grill hopper with apple-flavored wood pellets, power the grill on by using the control panel, select 'smoke' on the temperature dial, or set the temperature to 450 degrees F and let it preheat for a minimum of 15 minutes. Meanwhile, take a medium bowl, place peas in it, add garlic powder and oil, season with salt and black pepper, toss until mixed, then spread on the sheet pan. When the grill has preheated, open the lid, place the prepared sheet pan on the grill grate, shut the grill, and smoke for 10 minutes until slightly charred. Serve straight away.

Nutrition

Calories: 91 Cal Fat: 5 g

Carbs: 9 g Protein: 4 g Fiber: 3 g

Cauliflower with Parmesan and Butter

Preparation time: 15 minutes

Cooking time: 45 minutes

Servings: 4

Ingredients:

1 medium head of cauliflower

1 teaspoon minced garlic

1 teaspoon salt

½ teaspoon ground black pepper

1/4 cup olive oil

1/2 cup melted butter, unsalted

1/2 tablespoon chopped parsley

1/4 cup shredded parmesan cheese

Directions:

Switch on the Traeger grill, fill the grill hopper with flavored wood pellets, power the grill on by using the control panel, select 'smoke' on the temperature dial, or set the temperature to 450 degrees F and let it preheat for a minimum of 15 minutes.

Meanwhile, brush the cauliflower head with oil, season with salt and black pepper then place in a skillet pan.

When the grill has preheated, open the lid, place the prepared skillet pan on the grill grate, shut the grill, and smoke for 45 minutes until golden brown and the center has turned tender.

Meanwhile, take a small bowl, place melted butter in it, and then stir in garlic, parsley, and cheese until combined.

Baste cheese mixture frequently in the last 20 minutes of cooking and, when done, remove the pan from heat and garnish cauliflower with parsley.

Cut it into slices and then serve.

Nutrition

Calories: 128 Cal Fat: 7.6 g

Carbs: 10.8 g Protein: 7.4 g Fiber: 5 g

Grilled Carrots and Asparagus

Preparation time: 10 minutes

Cooking time: 30 minutes

Servings: 6

Ingredients:

1-pound whole carrots, with tops

1 bunch of asparagus, ends trimmed

Sea salt as needed

1 teaspoon lemon zest

2 tablespoons honey

2 tablespoons olive oil

Directions:

Switch on the Traeger grill, fill the grill hopper with flavored wood pellets, power the grill on by using the control panel, select 'smoke' on the temperature dial, or set the temperature to 450 degrees F and let it preheat for a minimum of 15 minutes.

Meanwhile, take a medium dish, place asparagus in it, season with sea salt, drizzle with oil and toss until mixed.

Take a medium bowl, place carrots in it, drizzle with honey, sprinkle with sea salt and toss until combined.

When the grill has preheated, open the lid, place asparagus and carrots on the grill grate, shut the grill, and smoke for 30 minutes.

When done, transfer vegetables to a dish, sprinkle with lemon zest then serve.

Nutrition

Calories: 79.8 Cal

Fat: 4.8 g

Carbs: 8.6 g

Protein: 2.6 g

Fiber: 3.5 g

Kale Chips

Preparation time: 10 minutes

Cooking time: 20 minutes

Servings: 6

Ingredients:

2 bunches of kale, stems removed

½ teaspoon of sea salt

4 tablespoons olive oil

Directions:

Switch on the Traeger grill, fill the grill hopper with apple-flavored wood pellets, power the grill on by using the control panel, select 'smoke' on the temperature dial, or set the temperature to 250 degrees F and let it preheat for a minimum of 15 minutes. Meanwhile, rinse the kale leaves, pat dry, spread the kale on a sheet tray, drizzle with oil, season with salt and toss until well coated. When the grill has preheated, open the lid, place sheet tray on the grill grate, shut the grill, and smoke for 20 minutes until crisp.

Serve straight away.

Nutrition

Calories: 110 Cal Fat: 5 g

Carbs: 15.8 g Protein: 5.3 g Fiber: 5.6 g

Bacon-Wrapped Jalapeño Poppers

Preparation Time: 15 min

Cooking Time: 40 min

Servings: 8 to 12

Ingredients:

12 large jalapeño peppers

8 oz cream cheese, softened

1 cup pepper jack cheese, shredded

Juice of 1 lemon 1/2 tsp garlic powder

1/4 tsp kosher salt

1/4 tsp ground black pepper

12 bacon slices, cut in half

Directions:

Preheat pellet grill to 400°F.

Slice jalapeños in half lengthwise. Remove seeds and scrape sides with a spoon to remove the membrane.

In a medium bowl, mix cream cheese, pepper jack cheese, garlic powder, salt, and pepper until thoroughly combined.

Use a spoon or knife to place the cream cheese mixture into each jalapeño half. Make sure not to fill over the sides of the jalapeño half.

Wrap each cheese-filled pepper with a half slice of bacon. If you can't get a secure wrap, then hold bacon and pepper together with a toothpick.

Place assembled poppers on the grill and cook for 15-20 minutes or until bacon is crispy.

Remove from the grill, allow to cool, then serve and enjoy!

Nutrition:

Calories: 78.8

Fat: 7.2 g

Cholesterol: 19.2 mg

Carbohydrate: 1 g

Fiber: 0.2 g

Sugar: 0.7 g

Protein: 2.5 g

Roasted Parmesan Cheese Broccoli

Preparation Time: 5 min

Cooking Time: 45 min

Servings: 3 to 4

Ingredients:

3 cups broccoli, stems trimmed

1 tbsp lemon juice

1 tbsp olive oil

2 garlic cloves, minced

1/2 tsp kosher salt

1/2 tsp ground black pepper

1 tsp lemon zest

1/8 cup parmesan cheese, grated

Directions:

Preheat pellet grill to 375°F.

Place broccoli in a resealable bag. Add lemon juice, olive oil, garlic cloves, salt, and pepper. Seal the bag and toss to combine. Let the mixture marinate for 30 minutes.

Pour broccoli into a grill basket. Place the basket on grill grates to roast. Grill broccoli for 14-18 minutes, flipping broccoli halfway through. Grill until tender yet a little crispy on the outside.

Remove broccoli from the grill and place on a serving dish—zest with lemon and top with grated parmesan cheese. Serve immediately and enjoy!

Nutrition:

Calories: 82.6

Fat: 4.6 g

Cholesterol: 1.8 mg

Carbohydrate: 8.1 g

Fiber: 4.6 g

Sugar: 0

Protein: 5.5

CHAPTER 16:

Lamb and Goat Recipes

Lamb Kabobs

Preparation Time: 8 minutes

Cooking Time: 35 minutes

Servings: 6

Ingredients:

1 ¼ cup of olive oil

1 ¼ cup of sherry

1 or 2 red onions, medium

1 Heaped tablespoon of GMG Wild Game Rub

1 Heaped tablespoon of ground black pepper

5 Garlic cloves

A leg of lamb

Directions:

Trim the fat from the lamb; then cut the lamb into cubes of about 1 ½ inch

Place in a large bowl; then sprinkle the rub over the meat and toss until your ingredients are very well combined

If you don't have an already prepared rub; just combine 1 teaspoon of brown sugar with 1 teaspoon of salt, ¼ teaspoon of turmeric; and ¼ teaspoon of ginger.

Peel the garlic and press to mash it

Chop the onion into rough dices in a small bowl; then chop a few sprigs of parsley

Add the liquid to the onion; then; mix and pour the mixture of the onion over the cubed lamb and place in the refrigerator for an overnight

Skewer the lamb chunks into wooden skewers

Grill the kabobs at a temperature of about 360-380° for about 25 to 35 minutes

Remove the meat from the grill

Serve and enjoy your dish!

Nutrition

Calories: 200,

Fat: 11g,

Protein: 22g

Grilled Pork chops

Preparation Time: 10 minutes

Cooking Time: 7 hours

Servings: 6

Ingredients:

For the Lamb

16 to 17 lamb chops

2 tablespoons of avocado oil

2 tablespoons of Greek Freak seasoning

For the Mint Sauce

1 cup of olive oil

10 to 12 garlic cloves

1 teaspoon of salt

¼ teaspoon of fresh ground black pepper

¼ teaspoon of dry oregano

¾ cup of lemon juice

1 tablespoon of chopped mint

1 tablespoon of chopped Italian parsley

Directions:

Start by placing the lamb chops in a bag with 1/3 cup of mint sauce; then let marinate for about 25 to 30 minutes

Remove from the marinade; then discard the sauce with the raw lamb

Preheat your Traeger grill to about 450°; then sprinkle the chops with the seasoning

Place the lamb chops on top of the grill.

Cook for about 3 to 4 minutes per side; then and remove to let rest before serving.

Serve and enjoy your dish!

Nutrition

Calories: 362, Fat: 26g,

Carbohydrates: 0 g,

Dietary Fiber: 0g,

Protein: 31g

Grilled Lamb liver

Preparation Time: 5 minutes

Cooking Time: 15 minutes

Servings: 3

Ingredients:

1 lb. of lamb liver; chopped into thin slices

½ Cup of olive oil

1 Crushed garlic clove

1 tbsp of fresh finely chopped mint

1 tsp of salt

¼ tsp of black pepper freshly ground

Directions:

Preheat a Traeger grill pan over medium-high heat.

Rinse the lamb liver thoroughly under cold running water.

Pat the liver dry with a clean paper towel; then using a sharp knife; remove the tough veins; then cut into thin slices

In a small bowl, combine the olive oil with the crushed garlic, the mint, the salt, and the pepper.

Mix very well until your ingredients are very well incorporated

Generously brush the slices of the liver with the mixture and grill for about 5 to 7 minutes on each of the sides.

Remove from the heat; then serve and enjoy!

Enjoy!

Nutrition

Calories: 141, Fat: 3.8g,

Carbohydrates: 0 g, Dietary Fiber: 0g,

Protein: 21.5g

Roasted Leg of Lamb

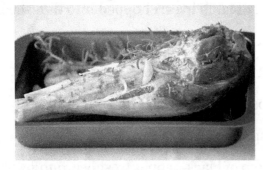

Preparation Time: 10 minutes

Cooking Time: 2 hours

Servings: 6

Ingredients:

2 teaspoons extra virgin olive oil

1 tablespoon crushed garlic

7 pounds bone-in leg of lamb

4 cloves of garlic, sliced lengthwise

4 sprig rosemary, cut into 1-inch pieces

2 lemons, sliced

Salt and pepper to taste

Directions:

Combine olive oil and crushed garlic. Rub the mixture on the leg of the lamb. Make small perforations in the lamb using a sharp knife and stuff the slivered garlic and rosemary sprigs. Zest and juice the lemons and sprinkle over the lamb. Season with salt and pepper to taste. When ready to cook, fire the Traeger Grill to 5000F. Use desired wood pellets when cooking. Close the lid and preheat for 15 minutes. Place the seasoned leg of lamb on the grill grate and reduce the grill to 3500F. Cook for 2 hours. Let the lamb rest for 15 minutes before carving.

Nutrition:

Calories per serving: 439;

Protein: 74.1g; Carbs: 2g; Fat: 14.9g

Sugar: 0.6g

Grilled Lamb Kabobs

Preparation Time: 10 minutes

Cooking Time: 16 minutes

Servings: 6

Ingredients:

½ cup olive oil

½ tablespoon salt

2 teaspoons black pepper

2 tablespoons chopped mint

½ tablespoon cilantro, chopped

1 teaspoon cumin

½ cup lemon juice

3 pounds boneless leg of lamb, cut into 2-inch cubes

15 apricots, halved and seeded

5 onions, cut into wedges

Directions:

In a bowl, combine the oil, salt, pepper, mint, cilantro, cumin, and lemon juice.

Massage the mixture onto the lamb shoulder and allow it to marinate in the fridge for at least 2 hours.

Remove the lamb from the marinade and thread the lamb, apricots, and red onion alternatingly on a skewer.

When ready to cook, fire the Traeger Grill to 4000F. Use desired wood pellets when cooking. Close the lid and preheat for 15 minutes.

Place the skewers on the grill grate and cook for 8 minutes on each side.

Remove from the grill.

Nutrition:

Calories per serving: 652;

Protein: 53.9g;

Carbs: 38.1g;

Fat: 31.8g

Sugar: 29.4g

Braised Lamb Shank

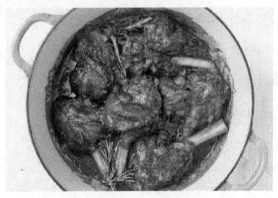

Preparation Time: 10 minutes

Cooking Time: 4 hours

Servings: 6

Ingredients:

6 whole lamb shanks

Traeger Prime Rib Rub

1 cup beef broth

1 cup red wine

4 sprig rosemary and thyme

Directions:

Season the lamb shanks with Traeger Prime Rib Rub.

When ready to cook, fire the Traeger Grill to 5000F. Use desired wood pellets when cooking. Close the lid and preheat for 15 minutes.

Place the lamb shanks directly on the grill grate and cook for 20 minutes or until the surface browns.

Transfer the shanks to a Dutch oven and pour in beef broth.

Place the Dutch oven back on the grill grate and reduce the temperature to 3250F. Cook for another 3 to 4 hours.

Nutrition:

Calories per serving: 532;

Protein: 55.2g;

Carbs: 10.2g;

Fat: 21.4g

Sugar: 2.3g

Smoked Lamb Leg with Salsa Verde

Preparation Time: 10 minutes

Cooking Time: 3 hours

Servings: 6

Ingredients:

2 tablespoons oil

1 whole leg of lamb, fat trimmed and cut into chunks

Salt to taste

6 cloves green garlic, unpeeled

1-pound tomatillos, husked and washed

1 small yellow onion, quartered

5 whole serrano chili peppers

1 tablespoon capers, drained

¼ cup cilantro, finely chopped

½ teaspoon sugar

1 cup chicken broth

3 tablespoons lime juice, freshly squeezed

Directions:

Fire the Traeger Grill to 5000F. Use desired wood pellets when cooking. Close the lid and preheat for 15 minutes.

Place a Dutch oven on the grill grate and add oil.

Put the lamb in the Dutch oven and season with salt to taste. Stir once then close the lid.

Place the garlic, tomatillos, onion, serrano peppers, and capers in a parchment-lined baking tray.

Season with salt to taste and drizzle with olive oil.

Place in the grill and cook for 15 minutes.

Remove the vegetables from the grill and transfer to a blender. Add cilantro and sugar.

Season with more salt if needed. Pulse until smooth then set aside.

Pour the mixture into the Dutch oven and add in chicken broth and lime juice.

Cook for 3 hours.

Nutrition:

Calories per serving: 430;

Protein: 56.4g;

Carbs: 7.8g;

Fat: 18.4g

Sugar: 3.9g

Grilled Lamb Chops with Rosemary

Preparation Time: 10 minutes

Cooking Time: 12 minutes

Servings: 4

Ingredients:

½ cup extra virgin olive oil

¼ cup coarsely chopped onion

2 cloves of garlic, minced

2 tablespoons soy sauce

2 tablespoons balsamic vinegar

1 tablespoon fresh rosemary

2 teaspoons Dijon mustard

1 teaspoon Worcestershire sauce

Salt and pepper to taste

4 lamb chops (8 ounces each)

Directions:

Heat oil in a saucepan over medium flame and sauté the onion and garlic until fragrant. Place in a food processor together with the soy sauce, vinegar, rosemary, mustard, Worcestershire sauce, salt, and pepper. Pulse until smooth. Set aside.

Fire the Traeger Grill to 5000F. Use desired wood pellets when cooking. Close the lid and preheat for 15 minutes. Brush the lamb chops on both sides with the paste. Place on the grill grates and cook for 6 minutes per side or until the internal temperature reaches 1350F for medium-rare. Serve with the paste if you have leftovers.

Nutrition:

Calories per serving: 442;

Protein: 16.7g;

Carbs: 6.1g;

Fat:38.5 g

Sugar: 3.7g

Bison Tomahawk Steak

Preparation Time: 10 minutes

Cooking Time: 12 minutes

Servings: 4

Ingredients:

2 ½ whole bone-in buffalo rib-eye steak

2 teaspoons cherrywood smoked salt

1 ½ tablespoon black pepper

Directions:

Fire the Traeger Grill to 4500F. Use desired wood pellets when cooking. Close the lid and preheat for 15 minutes.

Season the rib-eye steak with salt and pepper to taste.

Place the steak directly on the grill grate. Grill for 6 minutes on each side or until the internal temperature reaches 1400F.

Remove from the grill and allow to rest before slicing.

Nutrition:

Calories per serving: 751;

Protein: 51.6g; Carbs: 1.7g;

Fat: 60.1g; Sugar: 0.02g

Braised Elk Shank

Preparation Time: 10 minutes

Cooking Time: 4hour 10 minutes

Servings: 6

Ingredients:

3 elk shanks

Salt and pepper to taste

3 tablespoons canola oil

2 whole onions, halved

4 cloves of garlic, minced

2 dried bay leaves

2 cups red wine

1 sprig of rosemary

2 carrots, peeled and halved lengthwise

1 bunch fresh thyme

3 quarts beef stock

Directions:

Fire the Traeger Grill to 5000F. Use desired wood pellets when cooking. Place a cast-iron pan on the grill grate. Close the lid and preheat for 15 minutes.

Season the shanks with salt and pepper. Place canola oil in the heated cast iron and place the shanks. Close the grill lid and cook for five minutes on each side.

Add the onions and garlic and sauté for 1 minute.

Stir in the rest of the ingredients.

Close the grill lid and cook for 4 hours until soft.

Nutrition:

Calories per serving: 331;

Protein: 47.2g;

Carbs: 11.5g;

Fat: 11.2g

Sugar: 5.4g

Baked Venison Meatloaf

Preparation Time: 10 minutes

Cooking Time: 1 hour 30 minutes

Servings: 6

Ingredients:

2 pounds venison, ground

1-pound pork, ground

1 cup breadcrumbs

1 cup milk

2 tablespoons onion, diced

3 tablespoons salt

1 tablespoon black pepper

½ tablespoon thyme

1 ½ pounds parsnips, chopped

1 ½ pounds russet potatoes, chopped

¼ cup butter

Directions:

Fire the Traeger Grill to 500OF. Use desired wood pellets when cooking. Close the lid and preheat for 15 minutes.

Combine all ingredients in a bowl. Place the mixture in a greased loaf pan.

Place in the Traeger Grill and cook for 1 hour and 30 minutes or until the internal temperature reads at 160F.

Nutrition:

Calories per serving: 668;

Protein: 70.4g;

Carbs: 45.7 g;

Fat: 22g

Sugar: 8.7g

Roasted Venison Tenderloin

Preparation Time: 10 minutes

Cooking Time: 20 minutes

Servings: 4

Ingredients:

2 pounds venison

¼ cup dry red wine

2 cloves garlic, minced

2 tablespoons soy sauce

1 ½ tablespoon red wine vinegar

1 tablespoon rosemary

1 teaspoon black pepper

½ cup olive oil

Salt to taste

Directions:

Remove the membrane covering the venison. Set aside.

Mix the rest of the ingredients in a bowl. Place the venison in the bowl and allow to marinate for at least 5 hours in the fridge.

Fire the Traeger Grill to 5000F. Use desired wood pellets when cooking. Close the lid and preheat for 15 minutes.

Remove the venison from the marinade and pat dry using a paper towel.

Place on the grill grate and cook for 10 minutes on each side for medium-rare.

Nutrition:

Calories per serving: 611;

Protein: 68.4g; Carbs: 3.1g;

Fat: 34.4g Sugar: 1.6g

Grilled Venison Kabob

Preparation Time: 10 minutes

Cooking Time: 15 minutes

Servings: 6

Ingredients:

1 venison, blackstrap steaks cut into large cubes

2 whole red onion, quartered

2 whole green bell pepper, sliced into big squares

Oil as needs

Salt and pepper to taste

Directions:

Place all ingredients in a mixing bowl.

Toss to coat the meat and vegetables with the oil and seasoning.

Thread the meat and vegetables into metal skewers in an alternating manner.

Fire the Traeger Grill to 5000F.

Use desired wood pellets when cooking.

Close the lid and preheat for 15 minutes.

Place the kabobs on the grill grate and cook for 15 minutes.

Make sure to turn once halfway through the cooking time.

Remove from the grill and serve with yogurt if desired.

Nutrition:

Calories per serving: 267;

Protein: 32.4g;

Carbs: 10.1g;

Fat: 10.4g

Sugar: 4.8 g

Sweetheart Steak

Preparation Time: 10 minutes

Cooking Time: 14 minutes

Servings: 1

Ingredients:

20 ounces boneless strip steak, butterflied

2 ounces pure sea salt

2 teaspoons black pepper

2 tablespoons raw dark chocolate, finely chopped

½ tablespoon extra-virgin olive oil

Directions:

On a cutting board, trim the meat into a heart shape using a sharp knife. Set aside.

In a smaller bowl, combine the rest of the ingredients to create a spice rub mix.

Rub onto the steak and massage until well-seasoned.

When ready to cook, fire the Traeger Grill to 4500F. Use desired wood pellets when cooking. Close the lid and preheat for 15 minutes.

Grill the steak for 7 minutes on each side.

Allow resting for 5 minutes before slicing.

Nutrition:

Calories per serving: 727;

Protein: 132.7g; Carbs: 8.8 g;

 Fat: 18.5g

Sugar: 5.2g

Bloody Mary Flank Steak

Preparation Time: 10 minutes

Cooking Time: 14 minutes

Servings: 3

Ingredients:

2 cups Traeger Smoked Bloody Mary Mix or V8 Juice

 ½ cup vodka

1 whole lemon, juiced

3 cloves garlic, minced

1 tablespoon Worcestershire sauce

1 teaspoon ground black pepper

1 teaspoon celery salt

 ½ cup of vegetable oil

1 ½ pound flank steak

Directions:

Place all ingredients except for the flank steak in a bowl. Mix until well-combined.

Put the flank steak in a plastic bag and pour half of the marinade over. Marinate for at least 24 hours in the fridge. When ready to cook, fire the Traeger Grill to 5000F. Use desired wood pellets when cooking. Close the lid and preheat for 15 minutes. Drain the flank steak and pat dry using a paper towel. Place on the grill grate and cook for 7 minutes on each side. Meanwhile, place the remaining marinade (unused) in a saucepan and heat until the sauce thickens.

Once the steak is cooked, remove from the grill, and allow it to rest for 5 minutes before slicing.

Pour over the sauce.

Nutrition:

Calories per serving: 719;

Protein: 51.9g;

Carbs: 15.4g;

Fat: 51g

Sugar: 6.9g

Traeger Grill Rosemary lamb with garlic

Preparation Time: 10 minutes

Cooking Time: 10 minutes

Servings: 6

Ingredients:

2 Pounds of lamb loin or rib chops thick cut

4 Minced garlic cloves garlic

1 tablespoon of fresh chopped rosemary

1 and ¼ teaspoons of kosher salt

½ teaspoon of ground black pepper

The zest of 1 lemon

¼ Cup of olive oil

Directions:

Combine the rosemary with the garlic, the salt, the pepper, the lemon zest, and the olive oil in a measuring cup.

Pour the prepared marinade over the lamb chops and make sure to flip them over to cover it and let marinate in the refrigerator for about 1 hour

Grill the lamb chops over medium-high heat for about 7 to 10 minutes, or until the internal temperature reads about 135 degrees F.

Allow the lamb chops to rest on a plate covered with an aluminum foil for about 5 minutes before serving.

Nutrition

Calories: 171.5,

Fat: 7.8g,

Carbohydrates: 0.4 g,

Dietary Fiber: 0.1g,

Protein: 23.2g

Rack of Lamb

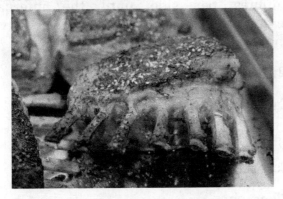

Preparation Time: 20 minutes

Cooking Time: 75 minutes

Servings: 4

Ingredients:

1/2 cup olive oil

½ cup dry mustard

¼ cup hot chili powder

2 tablespoons freshly squeezed lemon juice

2 tablespoon onion, minced

1 tablespoon paprika

1 tablespoon dried thyme

1 tablespoon salt

1 American rack of lamb, 7-9 chops

Mint Sauce

¼ cup fresh mint leaves, chopped

¼ cup hot water

2 tablespoons apple cider vinegar

2 tablespoons brown sugar

½ teaspoon salt

½ teaspoon fresh ground pepper

Directions:

Take a small bowl and mix in olive oil, mustard, chili powder, lemon juice, onion, paprika, thyme, Worcestershire sauce, salt

Preheat your smoker to 200 degrees F

Rub the paste all over the lamb and transfer to the smoker, smoke for 75 minutes until internal temperature reaches 145 degrees F

Remove lamb from heat and let it rest for a few minutes, serve with mint sauce

Enjoy!

Nutrition

Calories: 920

Fats: 83g

Carbs: 11g

Fiber: 1g

Mouthwatering Lamb Chops

Preparation Time: 15 minutes

Cooking Time: 20 minutes

Servings: 4

Ingredients:

For Marinade

½ cup of rice wine vinegar

1 teaspoon liquid smoke

2 tablespoons extra virgin olive oil

2 tablespoons dried onion, minced

1 tablespoon fresh mint, chopped

Lamb Chops

8 (4 ounces) lamb chops

½ cup hot pepper jelly

1 tablespoon Sriracha

1 teaspoon salt

1 teaspoon freshly ground black pepper

Directions:

Take a small bowl and whisk in rice wine vinegar, liquid smoke, olive oil, minced onion, and mint

Add lamb chops in an aluminum roasting pan, pour marinade over meat and turn well to coat

Cover with plastic wrap and marinate for 2 hours

Preheat your smoker to 165 degrees F

Take a small saucepan and place it over low heat, add hot pepper jelly and sriracha, keep it warm

Once ready to cook chops, remove them from marinade and pat dry

Discard marinade

Season chops with salt, pepper, and transfer to the grill grate

Close and smoke for 5 minutes

Remove chops from grill and increase the temperature to 450 degrees F

Transfer chops to grill and sear for 2 minutes per side until the internal temperature reaches 145 degrees F Serve chops and enjoy!

Nutrition

Calories: 227

Fats: 21g

Carbs: 0g

Fiber: 2g

Greek Lamb Leg

Preparation Time: 15 minutes

Cooking Time: 25 minutes

Servings: 12

Ingredients:

2 tablespoons fresh rosemary, chopped

1 tablespoon ground thyme

5 garlic cloves, minced

2 tablespoons salt

1 tablespoon fresh ground pepper

Butcher's string

1 whole boneless (6-8 pounds) leg of lamb

¼ cup extra virgin olive oil

1 cup red wine vinegar

½ cup canola oil

Directions:

Take a small bowl and add rosemary, thyme, garlic, salt, pepper and keep it on the side

Use butcher's string and tie leg of lamb in the shape of the roast

Rub lamb generously with olive oil mix and spice mix

Transfer to plate and cover with plastic wrap

Chill for 4 hours

Remove lamb from the fridge

Preheat your Smoker to 325 degrees F

Take a small bowl and add red wine vinegar and canola oil

Place lamb directly on the grill and close lid, smoke for 20-25 minutes per pound, making sure to keep basing after every 30 minutes

Once the thickest part reaches 145 degrees F, the lamb is ready

Let it rest for a while and serve

Enjoy!

Nutrition

Calories: 590

Fats: 50g

Carbs: 3g

Fiber: 1g

Moroccan Lamb Ribs

Preparation Time: 15 minutes

Cooking Time: 3 hours

Servings: 12

Ingredients:

2 racks lamb, membrane removed

Rub

2 tablespoons paprika

½ tablespoon coriander seeds

½ tablespoon salt

1 teaspoon cumin seeds

1 teaspoon ground allspice

1 teaspoon powdered lemon peel

½ teaspoon ground black pepper

Directions:

Preheat your smoker to 250 degrees F

Take a bowl and mix in paprika, coriander seeds, salt, cumin seeds, ground allspice, lemon peel, pepper, and using a mortar and pestle to grind

Season both sides of lamb

Transfer to your smoker and smoke for 3 hours until tender

Remove from smoker and serve

Enjoy!

Nutrition

Calories: 627

Fats: 24g

Carbs: 75g

Fiber: 3g

CHAPTER 17:

Pork Recipes

Smoked Baby Back Ribs

Preparation Time: 10 minutes

Cooking Time 2 hours

Servings: 6

Ingredients:

3 racks baby back ribs

Salt and pepper to taste

Directions:

Clean the ribs by removing the extra membrane that covers it. Pat dry the ribs with a clean paper towel. Season the baby back ribs with salt and pepper to taste. Allow resting in the fridge for at least 4 hours before cooking.

Once ready to cook, fire the Traeger Grill to 2250F. Use hickory wood pellets when cooking the ribs. Close the lid and preheat for 15 minutes.

Place the ribs on the grill grate and cook for two hours. Carefully flip the ribs halfway through the cooking time for even cooking.

Nutrition:

Calories per serving: 1037;

Protein: 92.5g;

Carbs: 1.4g;

Fat: 73.7g

Sugar: 0.2g

Smoked Apple Pork Tenderloin

Preparation Time: 10 minutes

Cooking Time: 3 hours

Servings: 6

Ingredients:

½ cup apple juice

3 tablespoons honey

3 tablespoons Traeger Pork and Poultry Rub

¼ cup brown sugar

2 tablespoons thyme leaves

½ tablespoons black pepper

2 pork tenderloin roasts, skin removed

Directions:

In a bowl, mix the apple juice, honey, pork and poultry rub, brown sugar, thyme, and black pepper. Whisk to mix everything.

Add the pork loins into the marinade and allow it to soak for 3 hours in the fridge.

Once ready to cook, fire the Traeger Grill to 2250F. Use hickory wood pellets when cooking the ribs. Close the lid and preheat for 15 minutes.

Place the marinated pork loin on the grill grate and cook until the temperature registers to 1450F. Cook for 2 to 3 hours on low heat.

Meanwhile, place the marinade in a saucepan. Place the saucepan in the grill and allow it to simmer until the sauce has reduced.

Before taking the meat out, baste the pork with the reduced marinade.

Allow resting for 10 minutes before slicing.

Nutrition:

Calories per serving: 203;

Protein: 26.4g; Carbs: 15.4g;

Fat: 3.6g

Sugar: 14.6g

Competition Style BBQ Pork Ribs

Preparation Time: 10 minutes

Cooking Time: 2 hours

Servings: 6

Ingredients:

2 racks of St. Louis-style ribs

1 cup Traeger Pork and Poultry Rub

1/8 cup brown sugar

4 tablespoons butter

4 tablespoons agave

1 bottle Traeger Sweet and Heat BBQ Sauce

Directions:

Place the ribs on the working surface and remove the thin film of connective tissues covering it. In a smaller bowl, combine the Traeger Pork and Poultry Rub, brown sugar, butter, and agave. Mix until well combined.

Massage the rub onto the ribs and allow them to rest in the fridge for at least 2 hours.

When ready to cook, fire the Traeger Grill to 2250F. Use desired wood pellets when cooking the ribs. Close the lid and preheat for 15 minutes.

Place the ribs on the grill grate and close the lid. Smoke for 1 hour and 30 minutes. Make sure to flip the ribs halfway through the cooking time.

Ten minutes before the cooking time ends, brush the ribs with BBQ sauce.

Remove from the grill and allow to rest before slicing.

Nutrition:

Calories per serving: 399;

Protein: 47.2g; Carbs: 3.5g;

Fat: 20.5g

Sugar: 2.3g

Smoked Apple BBQ Ribs

Preparation Time: 10 minutes

Cooking Time: 2 hours

Servings: 6

Ingredients:

2 racks St. Louis-style ribs

¼ cup Traeger Big Game Rub

1 cup apple juice

A bottle of Traeger BBQ Sauce

Directions:

Place the ribs on a working surface and remove the film of connective tissues covering it.

In another bowl, mix the Game Rub and apple juice until well-combined.

Massage the rub onto the ribs and allow them to rest in the fridge for at least 2 hours.

When ready to cook, fire the Traeger Grill to 2250F. Use apple wood pellets when cooking the ribs. Close the lid and preheat for 15 minutes.

Place the ribs on the grill grate and close the lid. Smoke for 1 hour and 30 minutes. Make sure to flip the ribs halfway through the cooking time.

Ten minutes before the cooking time ends, brush the ribs with BBQ sauce.

Remove from the grill and allow to rest before slicing.

Nutrition:

Calories per serving: 337

; Protein: 47.1g;

 Carbs: 4.7 g;

Fat: 12.9g

Sugar: 4g

Citrus-Brined Pork Roast

Preparation Time: 10 minutes

Cooking Time: 45 minutes

Servings: 6

Ingredients:

½ cup of salt

¼ cup brown sugar

3 cloves of garlic, minced

2 dried bay leaves

6 peppercorns

1 lemon, juiced

½ teaspoon dried fennel seeds

½ teaspoon red pepper flakes

½ cup of apple juice

½ cup of orange juice

5 pounds pork loin

2 tablespoons extra virgin olive oil

Directions:

In a bowl, combine the salt, brown sugar, garlic, bay leaves, peppercorns, lemon juice, fennel seeds, pepper flakes, apple juice, and orange juice.

Mix to form a paste rub.

Rub the mixture onto the pork loin and marinate for at least 2 hours in the fridge.

Add in the oil.

When ready to cook, fire the Traeger Grill to 300oF.

Use apple wood pellets when cooking.

Close the lid and preheat for 15 minutes.

Place the seasoned pork loin on the grill grate and close the lid.

Cook for 45 minutes.

Make sure to flip the pork halfway through the cooking time.

Nutrition:

Calories per serving: 869;

Protein: 97.2g;

Carbs: 15.2g;

Fat: 43.9g

Sugar: 13g

Pork Collar and Rosemary Marinade

Preparation Time: 15 minutes

Cooking Time: 30 minutes

Servings: 6

Ingredients:

1 pork collar, 3-4 pounds

3 tablespoons rosemary, fresh

3 shallots, minced

2 tablespoons garlic, chopped

½ cup bourbon

2 teaspoons coriander, ground

1 bottle of apple ale

1 teaspoon ground black pepper

2 teaspoons salt

3 tablespoons oil

Directions:

Take a zip bag and add pepper, salt, canola oil, apple ale, bourbon, coriander, garlic, shallots, rosemary, and mix well

Cut meat into slabs and add them to the marinade, let it refrigerate overnight

Preheat your smoker to 450 degrees F

Transfer meat to smoker and smoke for 5 minutes, lower temperature to 325 degrees F

Pour marinade all over and cook for 25 minutes more until the internal temperature reaches 160 degrees F

Serve and enjoy!

Nutrition

Calories: 420

Fats: 26g

Carbs: 4g

Fiber: 2g

Roasted Ham

Preparation Time: 15 minutes

Cooking Time:2 hours 15 minutes

Servings: 6

Ingredients:

8-10 pounds ham, bone-in

2 tablespoons mustard, Dijon

¼ cup horseradish

1 bottle BBQ Apricot Sauce

Directions:

Preheat your smoker to 325 degrees F

Cover a roasting pan with foil and place the ham, transfer to the smoker, and smoke for 1 hour and 30 minutes

Take a small pan and add sauce, mustard and horseradish, place it over medium heat and cook for a few minutes

Keep it on the side

After 1 hour 30 minutes of smoking, glaze ham and smoke for 30 minutes more until the internal temperature reaches 135 degrees F

Let it rest for 20 minutes, slice, and enjoy!

Nutrition

Calories: 460 Fats: 43g

Carbs: 10g Fiber: 1g

Smoked Pork Loin

Preparation Time: 15 minutes

Cooking Time: 3 hours

Servings: 6

Ingredients:

½ quart apple juice

½ quart apple cider vinegar

½ cup of sugar

¼ cup of salt

2 tablespoons fresh ground pepper

1 pork loin roast

½ cup Greek seasoning

Directions:

Take a large container and make the brine mix by adding apple juice, vinegar, salt, pepper, sugar, liquid smoke, and stir

Keep stirring until the sugar and salt have dissolved and added the loin

Add more water if needed to submerge the meat

Cover and chill overnight

Preheat your smoker to 250 degrees Fahrenheit with hickory wood

Coat the meat with Greek seasoning and transfer to your smoker

Smoker for 3 hours until the internal temperature of the thickest part registers 160 degrees Fahrenheit

Serve and enjoy!

Nutrition

Calories: 169

Fats: 5g

Carbs: 3g

Fiber: 3g

Smoke Pulled Pork

Preparation Time: 15 minutes

Cooking Time: 3 hours

Servings: 4

Ingredients:

Ingredients

6-9 lb. of whole pork shoulder

2 cups of apple cider

Big game rub

Directions

Set the temperature to 250 degrees F and put it on preheat by keeping the lid closed for 15 minutes

Now take off the excess fat from the butt of the pork and season it with big game rub on all sides

Put the pork butt on the grill grate making sure to keep the fat side up

Smoke it until the internal temperature reaches 160 degrees F. This should take approx. 3 to 5 hours

Remove it from the grill and keep aside

Now take a large baking sheet and keep 4 large pieces of aluminum foil one on top of the other. This should be wide enough to wrap the pork butt entirely

Keep the pork butt in the very center of the foil and bring up the sides a little

Pour apple cider on top of the pork and wrap the foil tightly around it

Keep it back on the grill again having the fat side up and cook till the internal temperature reaches 200 degrees F. This should take 3 to 4 hours approx.

Remove it from the grill and let it rest for 45 minutes inside the foil packet

Take off the foil and pour off the extra liquid

Now keep the pork in a dish and remove the bones and excess fat

Add the separated liquid back to the pork and season it again with big game rub

Serve and enjoy

Nutrition

Calories: 169 Fats: 5g

Carbs: 3g

Fiber: 3g

Easy Pork Chuck Roast

Preparation Time: 15 minutes

Cooking Time: 4 hours

Servings: 6

Ingredients:

1 whole 4-5 pounds chuck roast

¼ cup olive oil

¼ cup firm packed brown sugar

2 tablespoons Cajun seasoning

2 tablespoons paprika

2 tablespoons cayenne pepper

Directions:

Preheat your smoker to 225 degrees Fahrenheit using oak wood

Rub chuck roast all over with olive oil

Take a small bowl and add brown sugar, paprika, Cajun seasoning, cayenne

Coat the roast well with the spice mix

Transfer the chuck roast to smoker rack and smoke for 4-5 hours

Once the internal temperature reaches 165 degrees Fahrenheit, take the meat out and slice

Enjoy!

Nutrition

Calories: 219

Fats: 16g

Carbs: 0g

Fiber: 3g

Pineapple Pork BBQ

Preparation Time: 10 minutes

Cooking Time: 60 minutes

Servings: 4

Ingredients:

1-pound pork sirloin

4 cups pineapple juice

3 cloves garlic, minced

1 cup carne asada marinade

2 tablespoons salt

1 teaspoon ground black pepper

Directions:

Place all ingredients in a bowl. Massage the pork sirloin to coat with all ingredients. Place inside the fridge to marinate for at least 2 hours.

When ready to cook, fire the Traeger Grill to 3000F. Use desired wood pellets when cooking the ribs. Close the lid and preheat for 15 minutes.

Place the pork sirloin on the grill grate and cook for 45 to 60 minutes. Make sure to flip the pork halfway through the cooking time.

At the same time when you put the pork on the grill grate, place the marinade in a pan and place it inside the smoker. Allow the marinade to cook and reduce.

Baste the pork sirloin with the reduced marinade before the cooking time ends.

Allow resting before slicing.

Nutrition:

Calories per serving: 347;

Protein: 33.4 g;

Carbs: 45.8 g;

Fat: 4.2g

Sugar: 36g

BBQ Spareribs with Mandarin Glaze

Preparation Time: 10 minutes

Cooking Time: 60 minutes

Servings: 6

Ingredients:

3 large spareribs, membrane removed

3 tablespoons yellow mustard

1 tablespoon Worcestershire sauce

1 cup honey

1 ½ cup brown sugar

13 ounces Traeger Mandarin Glaze

1 teaspoon sesame oil

1 teaspoon soy sauce

1 teaspoon garlic powder

Directions:

Place the spareribs on a working surface and carefully remove the connective tissue membrane that covers the ribs.

In another bowl, mix the rest of the ingredients until well combined.

Massage the spice mixture onto the spareribs. Allow resting in the fridge for at least 3 hours.

When ready to cook, fire the Traeger Grill to 300oF.

Use hickory wood pellets when cooking the ribs.

Close the lid and preheat for 15 minutes.

Place the seasoned ribs on the grill grate and cover the lid.

Cook for 60 minutes.

Once cooked, allow resting before slicing.

Nutrition:

Calories per serving: 1263;

Protein: 36.9g;

Carbs: 110.3g;

Fat: 76.8g

Sugar: 107g

Smoked Pork Sausages

Preparation Time: 10 minutes

Cooking Time: 1 hour

Servings: 6

Ingredients:

3 pounds ground pork

½ tablespoon ground mustard

1 tablespoon onion powder

1 tablespoon garlic powder

1 teaspoon pink curing salt

1 teaspoon salt

1 teaspoon black pepper

¼ cup of ice water

Hog casings, soaked and rinsed in cold water

Directions:

Mix all ingredients except for the hog casings in a bowl. Using your hands, mix until all ingredients are well-combined.

Using a sausage stuffer, stuff the hog casings with the pork mixture.

Measure 4 inches of the stuffed hog casing and twist to form into a sausage. Repeat the process until you create sausage links.

When ready to cook, fire the Traeger Grill to 225oF. Use apple wood pellets when cooking the ribs. Close the lid and preheat for 15 minutes.

Place the sausage links on the grill grate and cook for 1 hour or until the internal temperature of the sausage reads at 155oF.

Allow resting before slicing.

Nutrition:

Calories per serving: 688;

Protein: 58.9g;

Carbs: 2.7g;

Fat: 47.3g

Sugar: 0.2g

Braised Pork Chile Verde

Preparation Time: 10 minutes

Cooking Time: 40 minutes

Servings: 6

Ingredients:

3 pounds pork shoulder, bone removed and cut into ½ inch cubes

1 tablespoon all-purpose flour

Salt and pepper to taste

1-pound tomatillos, husked and washed

2 jalapenos, chopped

1 medium yellow onion, peeled and cut into chunks

4 cloves of garlic

4 tablespoons extra virgin olive oil

2 cup chicken stock

2 cans green chilies

1 tablespoon cumin

1 tablespoon oregano

½ lime, juiced

¼ cup cilantro

Directions:

Place the pork shoulder chunks in a bowl and toss with flour. Season with salt and pepper to taste.

Use desired wood pellets when cooking. Place a large cast-iron skillet on the bottom rack of the grill. Close the lid and preheat for 15 minutes.

Place the tomatillos, jalapeno, onion, and garlic on a sheet tray lined with foil and drizzle with 2 tablespoon olive oil. Season with salt and pepper to taste.

Place the remaining olive oil in the heated cast iron skillet and cook the pork shoulder. Spread the meat evenly then close.

Before closing the lid, place the vegetables in the tray on the grill rack. Close the lid of the grill.

Cook for 20 minutes without opening the lid or stirring the pork. After 20 minutes, remove the vegetables from the grill and transfer to a blender. Pulse until smooth and pour into the pan with the pork. Stir in the chicken stock, green chilies, cumin, oregano, and lime juice. Season with salt and pepper to taste. Close the grill lid and cook for another 20 minutes. Once cooked, stir in the cilantro.

Nutrition:

Calories per serving: 389;

Protein: 28.5g; Carbs: 4.5g;

Fat: 24.3g Sugar: 2.1g

BBQ Pulled Pork Sandwiches

Preparation Time: 10 minutes

Cooking Time: 1 hour 30 minutes

Servings: 6

Ingredients:

8-10lbs of bone-in pork butt roast

12 Kaiser Rolls

1 cup of yellow mustard

Coleslaw

1 bottle of BBQ sauce

5 oz of sugar

Directions

Push the temperature to 225 degrees F and set your smoker to preheat

Now take out the pork roast from the packaging and keep it on a cookie sheet

Rub it thoroughly with yellow mustard

Now take a bowl and mix the BBQ sauce along with sugar in it

Use this mix to rub the roast thoroughly and give time for the rub to seep inside and melt in the meat

Now place this roast in the smoker and allow it to cook for 6 hours

When done, remove it from the smoker and

then wrap it in tin foil

Push the temperature to 250 degrees F and cook it for a couple of hours. The internal temperature should reach 200 degrees F

Let the pork butt rest in the foil for an hour before pulling it out

Now take the Kaiser roll and cut it into half

Mix the pulled pork with some BBQ sauce and pile on the top of each halved roll

Top it with coleslaw and serve

Nutrition:

Calories per serving: 426;

Protein: 65.3g;

Carbs: 20.4g;

Fat: 8.4g Sugar: 17.8g

Conclusion

Pellet grills are revolutionary and may forever change the way we cook.

These days, anyone can own a pellet grill since manufacturers meet the demand of clients from various backgrounds.

Modern pellet grills make cooking enjoyable and hassle-free.

It also eliminates guesswork thanks to the easy-to-follow recipes and the ability to remotely monitor and adjust your temperatures.

Whether you're an amateur home cook hosting a backyard cookout or a pit master at a barbecue competition, a wood pellet grill can easily become one of the most important appliances you can own to help you make flavorful meals with much less effort.

Although wood pellets grill isn't everyone's favorite choice, it's clear that a wood pellet grill is a must-have outdoor kitchen appliance. Whether you love smoking, grilling, roasting, barbecuing, or direct cooking of food, a wood pellet grill is versatile and has got you covered.

Cooking with a wood pellet grill allows you to choose the desired flavor of wood pellets to create the perfect smoke to flavor your food. Each wood pellet type has its personality and taste. The best part is you can use a single flavor or experiment with mixing and matching the flavors to invent your combination.

Just like any cooking appliance, wood pellets have some drawbacks but the benefits overshadow them. It is therefore definitely worth a try.

These days, one popular method of cooking is smoking, which many enthusiasts use. Proteins such as different kinds of meat, poultry, and fish would be ruined quickly if modern techniques in cooking are used. Smoking, on the other hand, is a process that takes a long time and low temperature, which thoroughly cooks the meat. The smoke, especially white smoke, greatly enhances the flavor of almost any food item. But more than that, smoking seals and preserves the nutrients in the food. Smoking is flexible and is one of the oldest techniques for making food.

Someone once dubbed smoking as a form of art. Only with a minimum period of consistent effort, any enthusiast can easily master the basics and advanced techniques. It is even said that once you master and improve on your expertise in smoking, you will not consider the other techniques in cooking to master anymore. But because of the many smoking techniques, you have to find a technique that is suitable for your temperament and style. You can do that by experimentation and trials of different smoking methods and different kinds of woods. Try cooking meat products for several hours using a heat source not directly on the meat. But you have to make sure that the smoke has a space to soak your meat and give it access way out. The picture of a good time with loved ones, neighbors, and friends having a backyard barbeque is a pretty sight, isn't it? Having a smoker-grill and some grilled and smoked recipes are excellent when you have visitors at home because you can deliver both tasty food and magical moments on a summer night, for example. Hundreds of awesome recipes are available that you can try with a wood pellet smoker-grill! Experiment, improve, or make your recipes – it is up to you. You can do it fast and easy. But if you want to be safe with the proven and tested ones, by all means, do so. These recipes have been known to be just right to the taste and they work every time. A combination of creating a correct impression the first time and every time and enjoying scrumptious food along the way will be your edge.

Another great thing about these recipes is that they are easy to prepare and do not require you to be a wizard in the kitchen. Simply by following a few easy steps and having the right ingredients at your disposal, you can use these recipes to make some delicious food in no time. So, try these recipes and spread the word! I'm sure this wood pellet smoker-grill recipe book will prove to be an invaluable gift to your loved ones, too!

Finally, while you will have fantastic smoking and grilling time with whichever wood pellet grill model you choose, the models are quite different. They hence offer different services and are suitable for different users. With new wood pellet grill series being produced each year, you need to shop smartly so that you buy a grill that perfectly fits you and meets all your needs.

If you are considering buying a grill yourself, then first you need to know the best kind of grills out in the market and what will suit you. You need to know how they work, compare, and which ones are trending. Traeger wood pellet grill is top on the markets and has many advantages over the standard cooking grill everyone has. New technology is coming out with better and better products to choose from, and if you don't upgrade your purchase and keep buying the same old stuff, then you will be left behind.

The Traeger grill provides a person with a great barbecuing experience with everyone, making food tastes better and cooking easier.

Now you no longer have to scour the web, hunting for your favorite wood pellet smoker-grill recipes. This book is a one-stop solution designed to eliminate all your struggles in finding the perfect wood pellet smoker-grill recipes for yourself and your loved ones.

CPSIA information can be obtained
at www.ICGtesting.com
Printed in the USA
BVHW011209131120
593255BV00014B/555